1000 FACTS ABOUT THE UNITED STATES OF AMERICA VOL. 3

Contents

"Ours is the only country deliberately founded on a good idea."

— John Gunther

Introduction

Welcome to the grand finale of our enlightening expedition, "1000 Facts about The United States of America vol. 3". This final installment of the series continues our journey through the intricate patchwork that forms the United States, a nation as diverse as it is captivating. Each page you turn, each fact you read, is a step further into the depth and breadth of a country that has endlessly fascinated the world.

Throughout this series, we've been unraveling the multilayered story of America, exploring its vibrant landscapes, unique cultures, illustrious history, and significant achievements across a range of domains. This final volume builds on that exploration, offering a wealth of information that enriches our understanding of this vast nation. From the geographical wonders that dot its land to the cultural nuances that distinguish each state, from its scientific feats to its sports triumphs, every fact unveils a new layer of the American narrative.

As we approach the end of this journey, it's essential to remember that while these facts provide fascinating insights into the nation's past and present, they also pave the way to a promising future. The United States continues to evolve, making history every day, and these facts capture just a snapshot of that dynamic journey.

This volume brings our exploration to a close, but the journey through the incredible tapestry of the United States is never truly over. For every fact you discover, there's always another waiting to amaze you, another story waiting to be told. Join us on this final leg of the journey, and let's celebrate the fascinating mosaic that is the United States of America.

Daniel Scott

Alabama

- **Music Hall of Fame:** The Alabama Music Hall of Fame in Tuscumbia celebrates Alabama's rich musical heritage.
- **Oldest Baseball Park:** Birmingham's Rickwood Field is the oldest professional baseball park in the U.S.
- **W.C. Handy Birthplace:** Florence, Alabama, is the birthplace of W.C. Handy, the "Father of the Blues."
- **Longest Yard Sale:** Alabama is one of the six states that partake in the annual 690-mile-long yard sale along the U.S. Route 127.
- **Unique State Beverage:** Alabama's official state beverage is Conecuh Ridge Whiskey, named after the brand's birthplace.
- **World's First Electric Trolley System:** Montgomery was the first city in the Western Hemisphere to implement city-wide electric street cars in 1886.
- **Rare Orchids:** Alabama's Bankhead National Forest is home to seven types of orchids not found anywhere else in the world.
- **Largest Brick Manufacturer:** Alabama is home to the largest brick manufacturer in the U.S., Jenkins Brick Company.
- **Barbecue Championship:** The annual Decatur Riverfest is Alabama's oldest barbecue championship, attracting competitors nationwide.
- **First 911 Call:** The first-ever 911 call in the United States was made in Haleyville, Alabama, in 1968.
- **Dinosaur Tracks:** Over 600 dinosaur tracks have been found in and near the town ofStevenson, marking the most significant such discovery in Alabama.
- **Southern Hospitality:** Monroeville, Alabama, is known as the "Literary Capital of Alabama" and inspired the setting for Harper Lee's "To Kill a Mockingbird."
- **Famed Bakers:** Dothan, Alabama, produces approximately 25% of the U.S.'s peanut crop and hosts the National Peanut Festival annually.

- **Historic Shipwreck:** The wreck of the Civil War ironclad USS Monitor lies in the Gulf of Mexico off the coast of Alabama.
- **Unclaimed Baggage:** Scottsboro, Alabama, is home to the Unclaimed Baggage Center, a store selling items from unclaimed airline luggage.
- **Coon Dog Cemetery:** Alabama houses the only cemetery in the world dedicated exclusively to coon dogs, a type of hunting dog.
- **Little River Canyon:** One of the deepest canyon systems east of the Mississippi River, Little River Canyon is located entirely atop Lookout Mountain in Alabama.
- **Camellia State:** Alabama's state flower is the camellia, not the native cotton plant as many believe.
- **Bird Lovers Paradise:** Dauphin Island, located in the Gulf of Mexico, is one of the top four locations in North America for viewing spring bird migrations.
- **Ave Maria Grotto:** Cullman, Alabama, is home to the Ave Maria Grotto, a four-acre park providing a garden setting for 125 miniature reproductions of some of the world's most famous religious structures.

Alaska

- **Northern Lights Research:** Poker Flat Research Range in Alaska is the world's largest land-based rocket research range and studies the Northern Lights.
- **Salmon Capital:** Ketchikan, Alaska, is known as the "Salmon Capital of the World."
- **Amber Discoveries:** Alaska is rich in amber, which often contains prehistoric insect inclusions over 90 million years old.
- **Arctic Research:** The University of Alaska Fairbanks is a world leader in Arctic research.
- **Migratory Birds:** Every spring, millions of migratory birds flock to Alaska's Copper River Delta.
- **Moose Popularity:** Alaska has more moose per square mile than any other U.S. state.
- **Fur Rendezvous:** Anchorage's annual Fur Rendezvous winter festival includes a popular dogsled race, the Rondy World Championship Sled Dog Race.
- **Quirky Law:** It's illegal to whisper in someone's ear while they're moose hunting in Alaska.
- **Dog Breed Origin:** The Alaskan Malamute dog breed originated in Alaska and was named after the native Inuit tribe Mahlemiut.
- **Alaska Native Heritage Center:** The Alaska Native Heritage Center in Anchorage educates visitors about Alaska's 11 distinct cultural groups.
- **Wildlife Conservation:** The Alaska Wildlife ConservationCenter is home to orphaned and injured animals and educates visitors on Alaska's wildlife.
- **Rainforest in Alaska:** The Tongass National Forest is the largest temperate rainforest in the United States.
- **Land of Lakes:** Alaska has over 3 million lakes, more than any other state.

- **Remarkable Wilderness:** Wrangell-St. Elias National Park and Preserve in Alaska is the largest national park in the United States.
- **Volcano Alley:** Alaska's Aleutian Islands have 57 volcanoes and are a significant part of the Pacific Ring of Fire.
- **Dinosaur Traces:** On Alaska's North Slope, dinosaur tracks have been discovered that date back to the Late Cretaceous period.
- **A Mammoth Discovery:** Fossilized remains of the woolly mammoth have been discovered in Alaska, hinting at the state's prehistoric past.
- **Arctic Man:** The Arctic Man Ski and Sno-Go Classic, a unique race involving snowmobiles and skiers, draws thousands to Alaska every year.
- **Frozen Ground:** A large part of Alaska's ground is permafrost, ground that remains frozen throughout the year.
- **Glacier Bay National Park:** Glacier Bay National Park in Alaska is a 3.3 million acre treasure of natural wonders and wildlife near Juneau.

Arizona

- **Montezuma Castle:** This well-preserved cliff dwelling was built by the Sinagua people between approximately 1100 and 1425 AD.
- **Olive Trees:** Arizona's climate is ideal for olive trees; the state has over 6,000 acres of groves.
- **World's Largest Rose:** The world's largest rose bush is located in Tombstone; its canopy covers over 8,000 square feet.
- **Gem Silica:** Arizona is the world's leading producer of the beautiful gem silica, a rare type of quartz.
- **Fort Huachuca:** This fort, established in 1877, was a key player in the Apache Wars and is now a National Historic Landmark.
- **Arizona-Sonora Desert Museum:** This fusion experience includes a zoo, botanical garden, art gallery, natural history museum, and aquarium.
- **Apache Trout:** The Apache Trout, found only in Arizona, is the state's official fish.
- **Arizona State University:** ASU, founded in 1885, is one of the largest public universities by enrollment in the U.S.
- **Jerome, the Billion Dollar Copper Camp:** Once known as the wickedest town in the West, Jerome was a copper mining camp, growing from a settlement of tents to a roaring mining community.
- **Biltmore Estate:** The Arizona Biltmore, often referred to as the "Jewel of the Desert," was partially designed by Frank Lloyd Wright.
- **Arcosanti:** The experimental town Arcosanti in central Arizona blends architecture and ecology and is a designated Arizona Historic Site.
- **Bell Rock Vortex:** Bell Rock in Sedona is said to be a site of a powerful energy vortex.
- **Taliesin West:** Architect Frank Lloyd Wright's winter home and school in Scottsdale.

- **Asteroid Discovery:** The first asteroid to be discovered from an observatory in the U.S. was at Lowell Observatory in Flagstaff, Arizona.
- **Palo Verde Nuclear Generating Station:** The largest nuclear power plant in the U.S. is located in Arizona.
- **Hopi Reservation:** The Hopi Reservation, for the Hopi and Arizona Tewa people, is entirely surrounded by the larger Navajo Reservation.
- **Chiricahua National Monument:** Known as the "Land of Standing-Up Rocks" by the Apache, its unique rock formations attract visitors worldwide.
- **Hohokam Pima National Monument:** This monument protects an ancient Hohokam village known as "Snaketown."
- **Roosevelt Dam:** At the time of its completion in 1911, it was the largest masonry dam in the world.
- **Titan II Missile Museum:** The last remaining Titan II site open to the public, offering a dramatic glimpse of the Cold War era.

Arkansas

- **Home of the Bowie Knife:** The famous Bowie knife was created by James Black in the early 1830s for Jim Bowie, a notorious knife fighter.
- **Fayetteville Farmers Market:** The Farmers Market at the Fayetteville Square has been ranked among America's best farmers' markets.
- **Dinosaur Discoveries:** The first dinosaur tracks found in Arkansas were discovered in a gypsum mine in Nashville in 1983.
- **Kerr's American Holly:** The state tree of Arkansas, known for its rich foliage and bright red berries.
- **Annual Bean Fest:** Each year, Mountain View holds a Bean Fest where thousands of pounds of beans are cooked in traditional iron kettles.
- **Fort Smith National Historic Site:** This site includes the remains of two frontier forts and the Federal Court for the Western District of Arkansas.
- **The Hemingway-Pfeiffer Museum:** Nobel Prize-winning author Ernest Hemingway wrote portions of his most famous works in Piggott, Arkansas.
- **Arkansas Alligator Farm and Petting Zoo:** This is one of the oldest alligator farms in the country and includes a petting zoo.
- **Woolly Hollow State Park:** This park is home to one of the best preserved log cabins in Arkansas, built in the 1880s.
- **Bathhouse Row:** A collection of bathhouses, associated buildings, and gardens located at Hot Springs National Park.
- **The Great Passion Play:** In Eureka Springs, this outdoor drama is one of the most attended in the U.S., telling the story of Christ's last days.
- **Meteorite Impact Site:** The city of Delight is home to an ancient meteorite impact site, discovered in the 20th century.

- **Famous Writers:** Maya Angelou, a renowned writer and civil rights activist, spent much of her childhood in Stamps, Arkansas.
- **White River Monster:** Since the early 20th century, reports of a large, unknown aquatic creature living in the White River have circulated.
- **Arkansas Arts Center:** This center in Little Rock is the state's largest cultural institution, housing a renowned collection of international art.
- **Weiner Dog Races:** Every year, the town of Weiner hosts the Arkansas Dachshund Races, attracting entrants from across the state.
- **Home to Multiple Fortune 500 Companies:** Arkansas is the headquarters for multiple Fortune 500 companies, including Walmart, Tyson Foods, and J.B. Hunt.
- **Ouachita Mountains:** These are the only mountains that run east to west rather than north to south in the United States.
- **The Duck Capital:** Stuttgart, Arkansas is considered the Duck and Rice Capital of the World and hosts an annual Wings Over the Prairie Festival.
- **Cotton Industry:** Arkansas is one of the leading cotton producing states in the U.S., contributing significantly to the textile industry.

California

- **California Roll:** This popular sushi roll was invented in Los Angeles in the 1960s, turning sushi into a global phenomenon.
- **Monarch Butterfly Migration:** Each winter, millions of monarch butterflies migrate to groves along the California coast.
- **Charles Schulz's Peanuts:** Cartoonist Charles Schulz, creator of the famous comic strip "Peanuts," lived and worked in Santa Rosa, California.
- **The California Red-Legged Frog:** This is the official state amphibian, made famous by Mark Twain in his short story "The Celebrated Jumping Frog of Calaveras County."
- **Big Sur:** This rugged and mountainous section of the Pacific coastline offers some of the most breathtaking coastal views in the world.
- **Prehistoric Fossils:** La Brea Tar Pits in Los Angeles is one of the world's most famous fossil sites, showcasing the Ice Age.
- **Joshua Tree National Park:** Named for its distinctive trees, this desert park offers unique landscapes and is a haven for rock climbers.
- **Giant Dipper Roller Coaster:** Located in Santa Cruz Beach Boardwalk, it's one of the oldest wooden roller coasters in the U.S.
- **State Marine Mammal:** The California gray whale, which migrates along the state's coast, is the official state marine mammal.
- **Olympic Games Host:** Los Angeles has hosted the Summer Olympic Games twice, in 1932 and 1984, and is set to host again in 2028.
- **Home to Many Celebrities:** Due to Hollywood, California is home to many film, television, and music celebrities.
- **The Sundial Bridge:** Located in Redding, this unique pedestrian bridge is also a working sundial, the world's largest.

- **The California Condor:** One of the world's rarest birds, it's the official state bird and represents a successful species recovery story.
- **Sutter's Mill:** The discovery site that sparked the California Gold Rush is now a historical landmark in Coloma.
- **Famous Parks:** California is home to nine national parks, more than any other state in the U.S.
- **Population Size:** California is the most populous state in the U.S., with a population greater than many countries.
- **Sonoma and Napa Valleys:** Renowned for their wineries and vineyards, they're among the premier wine regions in the world.
- **Palm Springs Modernism:** Known for its mid-century modern architecture, Palm Springs is a hub for design enthusiasts.
- **Venice Beach:** Famous for its bohemian spirit, skate park, and beachside gym known as Muscle Beach.
- **Lake Tahoe:** Straddling the California-Nevada border, it's known for its clear waters and surrounding ski resorts.

Colorado

- **The Broadmoor:** A luxury resort in Colorado Springs, it's the longest-running consecutive winner of both the AAA Five-Diamond and Forbes Five-Star awards.
- **Kersey Valley Spookywoods:** One of America's longest-running and largest Halloween attractions, located in Archdale.
- **Durango & Silverton Narrow Gauge Railroad:** A 3.5-foot narrow-gauge heritage railroad that operates 45.2 miles of track between Durango and Silverton.
- **Cliff Palace:** Located in Mesa Verde National Park, it's the largest cliff dwelling in North America.
- **The Denver Omelette:** A beloved breakfast dish that originated in Colorado, featuring ham, onions, and bell peppers.
- **Rocky Ford Cantaloupes:** Known as the sweetest cantaloupes around, they're grown in the Rocky Ford region of Colorado.
- **Celestial Seasonings:** One of the largest specialty tea manufacturers in North America, located in Boulder.
- **The National Western Stock Show:** A livestock show, horse show, and rodeo held each January in Denver, drawing crowds from all over.
- **Buckhorn Exchange:** Denver's oldest restaurant, it's renowned for its wild game dishes and Old West memorabilia.
- **The Unsinkable Molly Brown:** A survivor of the Titanic, she was a philanthropist and women's rights activist from Denver.
- **Telluride Bluegrass Festival:** An annual 4-day festival that draws some of the biggest names in bluegrass music.
- **Vail Ski Resort:** One of the largest ski resorts in the world, it's a major destination for winter sports enthusiasts.
- **The Historic Brown Palace Hotel:** Located in Denver, it's played host to presidents, prime ministers, and celebrities since 1892.
- **Kit Carson County Carousel:** A historic carousel in Burlington, it's the oldest wooden merry-go-round in the U.S.

- **Clyfford Still Museum:** Located in Denver, it's dedicated to the life and work of abstract expressionist painter Clyfford Still.
- **Garden of the Gods:** A public park located in Colorado Springs, it's famous for its stunning red sandstone formations.
- **Animas River:** Known for its Gold Medal fly-fishing waters and its significant role in Southwestern Colorado's culture and history.
- **Skiing Hall of Fame:** Located in Vail, it honors the athletes and pioneers who have significantly impacted American skiing.
- **Bishop Castle:** Built by one man, Jim Bishop, this unique stone and iron fortress includes a grand ballroom and a fire-breathing dragon.
- **Molly Brown House Museum:** Located in Denver, it explores the life of Titanic survivor Molly Brown and the Victorian era in which she lived.

Connecticut

- **I-95:** The longest north-south interstate in the U.S., it spans the entire length of Connecticut's coastline.
- **First Color Television:** The technology for color TV was developed in Connecticut by John Logie Baird in the 1940s.
- **First Cookbook:** The first American cookbook, American Cookery, was published in Hartford in 1796 by Amelia Simmons.
- **Knowlton Brothers paper mill:** Established in 1852 in the town of Vernon, it was the first to produce book paper from wood pulp in the U.S.
- **Elizabeth Park Rose Garden:** Located in Hartford, it's the third-largest rose garden in the country and has over 800 varieties of roses.
- **Connecticut State Capitol:** Located in Hartford, this beautiful building is made of marble and granite and topped by a gold leaf dome.
- **Devil's Hopyard State Park:** Despite its sinister name, this is a beautiful park known for its picturesque waterfalls and hiking trails.
- **First Sewing Machine:** The Howe Sewing Machine Company of Bridgeport, Connecticut, produced the first practical sewing machines.
- **West Cornwall Covered Bridge:** One of the last historic covered bridges in Connecticut, it spans the Housatonic River and is a popular photographic spot.
- **Submarine Force Museum:** Located in Groton, it's the only submarine museum operated by the U.S. Navy, and is home to the historic ship Nautilus.
- **Bushnell Park:** Located in Hartford, it's the oldest publicly funded park in the U.S.

- **Essex Steam Train & Riverboat:** Offers unique rail and boat excursions along the Connecticut River Valley, featuring vintage locomotives and riverboats.
- **Ivoryton Playhouse:** Founded in 1930, it's one of the oldest continuously operated professional summer theatres in the U.S.
- **Greenwich Polo Club:** One of the most elite high-goal polo venues in the world, it's been hosting matches since 1981.
- **Bleachery Dam:** The second largest waterfall by volume in Connecticut, it was once used to power an industrial bleachery.
- **Foxwoods Resort Casino:** One of the largest casinos in the world, it's owned and operated by the Mashantucket Pequot Tribal Nation.
- **The Glass House:** Designed by Philip Johnson in 1949, this iconic example of modernist architecture is now a National Trust Historic Site.
- **Sleeping Giant State Park:** Features two miles of mountaintop resembling a large human figure lying in repose, the "sleeping giant."
- **Hartford Whalers:** The former professional hockey team from Hartford, they moved to North Carolina in 1997 but are fondly remembered.
- **First Nuclear-Powered Submarine:** The USS Nautilus, built in 1954, was the world's first nuclear-powered submarine and is now a museum ship in Groton.

Delaware

- **USS Delaware:** A U.S. Navy battleship used during WWI, it was the lead ship of its class.
- **Mount Cuba Center:** A botanical garden dedicated to native plant species and ecological gardening.
- **Wilmington State Parks:** A collection of city parks in Wilmington, they offer a green oasis in the urban landscape.
- **C&D Canal:** The Chesapeake & Delaware Canal is a vital waterway connecting the Delaware River to the Chesapeake Bay.
- **American Discovery Trail:** This coast-to-coast trail runs right through Delaware, the only state it traverses entirely from border to border.
- **Delaware Symphony Orchestra:** One of the oldest symphony orchestras in the U.S., it's been performing since 1906.
- **Delaware State Forest:** This forest area is known for its wide variety of wildlife, recreational opportunities, and beautiful views.
- **Jungle Jim's River Safari Water Park:** A popular family attraction, it's the largest water park in Delaware.
- **Holy Trinity Church:** Also known as Old Swedes Church, it's the oldest church in the U.S. that's still in use and standing as originally built.
- **Great Cypress Swamp:** The largest freshwater wetland in the state, it's a vital habitat for birds and other wildlife.
- **Delaware Children's Museum:** This interactive museum in Wilmington is dedicated to helping children learn through play.
- **Winterthur Country Estate:** The childhood home of collector and horticulturist Henry Francis du Pont, it's now a museum of American decorative arts.
- **Delaware Blue Coats:** The NBA G League affiliate of the Philadelphia 76ers, based in Wilmington.

- **Old New Castle:** This well-preserved colonial city offers a step back in time with its cobbled streets and historic buildings.
- **Delaware Contemporary:** This non-collecting contemporary art museum in Wilmington is known for its 7 rotating exhibition galleries and 26 on-site artist studios.
- **Hagley Powder Yard:** The original gunpowder works at the DuPont Company's earliest mills, it's now part of the Hagley Museum.
- **Beaches:** Despite its small size, Delaware is home to several beautiful beaches along its Atlantic coast.
- **John Dickinson Plantation:** The home of John Dickinson, one of the Founding Fathers, is now a museum.
- **Delaware Bay:** It's one of the largest and most productive estuarine systems in the U.S., known for its shellfish and waterfowl.
- **Wilmington Trust:** Founded in 1903, this company has been a significant player in international banking and American finance.

Florida

- **Fort Lauderdale's Beaches:** Known for their excellent surf conditions and being a major spring break destination.
- **Walt Disney World Resort:** At 40 square miles, it's roughly the size of San Francisco or two Manhattan islands.
- **Daytona 500:** One of the most prestigious races in NASCAR, held annually at the Daytona International Speedway.
- **Palm Beach County:** It's larger than the whole of Rhode Island and has more golf courses than any other county in the U.S.
- **The Miami Seaquarium:** One of the oldest oceanariums in the U.S., it's home to a wide variety of marine species, including killer whales.
- **South Beach Diet:** A popular diet developed by Miami cardiologist Arthur Agatston, named after the glamorous area of Miami Beach.
- **Naples Zoo:** A nationally accredited zoo and historic tropical garden in Naples, Florida.
- **Florida's Coral Reefs:** The Florida Reef is the only living coral barrier reef in the continental U.S., and the third-largest coral barrier reef system in the world.
- **Panama City Beach:** Known for its 27-mile stretch of white-sand beaches and clear, emerald-green waters.
- **Mallory Square:** A plaza located in the city of Key West, known for its daily celebration of the sunset.
- **Blue Angels:** The U.S. Navy's flight demonstration squadron is based at Naval Air Station Pensacola.
- **Florida's Highways:** Florida has the longest system of state roads (followed by Texas) and interstate highways in the U.S.
- **Vizcaya Museum and Gardens:** This Miami estate includes extensive Italian Renaissance gardens and a historic village outbuildings compound.

- **Big Cypress National Preserve:** The first National Preserve in the National Park System, located in southern Florida.
- **Florida's Retirement Community:** Known as a popular retirement destination due to its warm climate and tax-friendly policies.
- **Palm Beach:** Known for its glitzy estates and its beaches, including the long, sandy Palm Beach Municipal Beach.
- **Ginnie Springs:** Known for its clear blue waters, the privately owned park allows camping and river tubing.
- **Florida Citrus Sports:** A not-for-profit events organizer, known for hosting the annual Citrus Bowl in Orlando.
- **Amelia Island:** Known for its luxury resorts, golf courses, and sandy beaches.
- **NASCAR:** The world-renowned stock car racing organization is headquartered in Daytona Beach, Florida.

Georgia

- **Juliette Gordon Low:** The founder of the Girl Scouts of the USA was born in Savannah in 1860.
- **R.E.M.:** This influential rock band was formed in Athens, Georgia, in 1980.
- **The Varsity:** An iconic restaurant chain headquartered in Atlanta, known as the world's largest drive-in.
- **The Big Chicken:** A famous landmark in Marietta, it's a 56-foot-tall steel-sided structure designed in the shape of a chicken.
- **Blue Ridge Mountains:** The state's northernmost part is in the Blue Ridge Mountains, part of the Appalachian Mountains system.
- **Callaway Gardens:** A 6,500-acre resort complex located in Pine Mountain, offering a range of outdoor activities.
- **Georgia State Capitol:** An architectural and historical treasure, the capitol building in Atlanta was completed in 1889.
- **Sweetwater Creek State Park:** A peaceful tract of wilderness only minutes from downtown Atlanta.
- **Allman Brothers Band:** This influential group was formed in Macon, Georgia, in 1969.
- **Georgia Peanuts:** The state produces nearly half of the total U.S. peanut crop.
- **Atlanta's Hartsfield-Jackson Airport:** Recognized as the world's busiest airport by passenger traffic since 1998.
- **Sapelo Island:** This barrier island on the Atlantic coast is notable for its historic Gullah community of Hog Hammock.
- **Amicalola Falls:** At 729 feet, it's the highest waterfall in Georgia and one of the highest cascades in the Eastern U.S.
- **Chattahoochee River:** This important waterway in the Southeastern U.S. begins in northeastern Georgia.
- **Ray Charles:** This influential musician, often referred to as "The Genius," was born in Albany, Georgia, in 1930.

- **Driftwood Beach:** This picturesque beach on Jekyll Island is known for its weathered, sun-bleached trees and branches.
- **Tallulah Gorge:** One of the most dramatic canyons in the eastern U.S., it's two miles long and nearly 1,000 feet deep.
- **Helen, Georgia:** This mountain town in northeastern Georgia is known for its Bavarian-style buildings.
- **Ellijay, Georgia:** Known as the "Apple Capital of Georgia" and hosts the annual Georgia Apple Festival.
- **Ty Cobb:** This baseball legend, often considered one of the greatest players, was born in Narrows, Georgia, in 1886.

Hawaii

- **State Insect:** The Kamehameha Butterfly, native to Hawaii, is the official state insect.
- **Molokini Crater:** This partially submerged volcanic crater off the coast of Maui is a popular destination for snorkeling and scuba diving.
- **Hawaiian Spinner Dolphins:** These dolphins, known for their acrobatic displays, are commonly seen in the waters around the islands.
- **Bishop Museum:** Located in Honolulu, this museum houses the largest collection of Polynesian cultural artifacts and natural history specimens in the world.
- **Kilauea Iki Crater Hike:** This popular trail in Hawaii Volcanoes National Park takes hikers across the still-steaming floor of Kilauea Iki Crater.
- **Hanalei Bay:** Located on Kauai, this bay is known for its stunning mountain views and crescent-shaped beach.
- **Hawaiian Green Sea Turtles:** These turtles, known as "honu" in Hawaiian, are a symbol of good luck and longevity.
- **Hawaiian Shirt Day:** June 28th is National Hawaiian Shirt Day, celebrating this iconic garment's impact on fashion worldwide.
- **Waipio Valley:** Also known as the "Valley of the Kings," this place on the Big Island was the residence of many early Hawaiian rulers.
- **Haiku Stairs:** Known as the "Stairway to Heaven," this steep hiking trail on Oahu offers extraordinary views but is officially closed to the public.
- **Iao Valley State Monument:** This park on Maui is home to the iconic 1,200-foot Iao Needle and was the site of a significant battle in Hawaiian history.
- **Macadamia Nuts:** These nuts were first planted in Hawaii in 1881, and the state is now a leading producer of macadamias.

- **Banyan Trees:** The state is home to several enormous, historic banyan trees, including the Lahaina Banyan in Maui that covers nearly an acre.
- **Whale Watching:** Each winter, thousands of humpback whales migrate to Hawaii's warm waters, making it a prime location for whale watching.
- **Hawaiian Poi:** This traditional Hawaiian dish is made from the fermented root of the taro plant.
- **Papakōlea Beach:** One of only four green sand beaches in the world is located in Hawaii, thanks to a mineral called olivine.
- **Waimanalo Bay:** Known for its turquoise water and powdery white sand, it's often ranked among the best beaches in the U.S.
- **Pali Lookout:** This site on Oahu provides panoramic views of the windward coast and was the location of a decisive battle in Hawaiian history.
- **Lanikai Beach:** Known for its clear water and white sand, it's consistently ranked among the world's best beaches.
- **Haleiwa Town:** This historic surf town on Oahu's North Shore is known for its laid-back vibe and big wave surf spots.

Idaho

- **Sun Valley Film Festival:** This annual event attracts filmmakers and celebrities from around the world.
- **Basque Festival:** Jaialdi, a festival celebrating Basque culture, takes place in Boise every five years.
- **Largest Man-Made Geyser:** Soda Springs is home to the only captive geyser in the world, which erupts every hour on the hour.
- **Idaho Potato Museum:** Located in Blackfoot, this unique museum celebrates the state's most famous crop.
- **Hot Springs:** The state has more usable hot springs than any other state in the U.S.
- **State Motto:** "Esto Perpetua" is the state motto and it means "Let it be Perpetual" or "It is forever".
- **Moose Population:** Idaho is home to one of the largest moose populations in the lower 48 states.
- **Evel Knievel's Jump:** In 1974, daredevil Evel Knievel attempted to jump the Snake River Canyon in Twin Falls using a steam-powered rocket.
- **State Fish:** The Cutthroat Trout is the state fish and known for the distinctive red coloration on the underside of its jaw.
- **Gold Rush:** Idaho City was once the largest city in the Pacific Northwest during the Gold Rush in the 1860s.
- **Famous Author:** Edgar Rice Burroughs, creator of Tarzan, lived in Idaho during the gold rush days.
- **Idaho's Tallest Building:** The U.S. Bank Building in Boise is the tallest building in the state.
- **Lewis and Clark Expedition:** The explorers Meriwether Lewis and William Clark traveled through Idaho in 1805 on their journey to the Pacific Ocean.
- **First Ski Resort:** Sun Valley was the first winter resort to install a chairlift in 1936.

- **Famous Actress:** Lana Turner, known as one of Hollywood's most glamorous stars, was born in the small mining town of Wallace.
- **Idaho State Bison Herd:** The state manages its own bison herd, which can be seen at the Wildlife Canyon Scenic Byway.
- **Galena Summit:** This summit in the Sawtooth Range offers some of the best views in the state.
- **Dog Bark Park Inn:** This bed and breakfast in Cottonwood is shaped like a giant beagle, earning it the nickname "Sweet Willy."
- **Idaho's Wine Country:** The Snake River Valley is Idaho's primary wine-producing region, with over 50 wineries.
- **Famous Dancer:** Renowned dancer Isadora Duncan was a resident of Idaho Springs.

Illinois

- **Joliet Prison:** This prison, made famous by the film "The Blues Brothers," opened in 1858 and closed in 2002.
- **Illinois Waterway:** This 336-mile waterway provides a shipping connection from the Great Lakes to the Gulf of Mexico.
- **The Magnificent Mile:** This upscale section of Michigan Avenue in Chicago is known for its luxury boutiques and landmarks.
- **Morton Arboretum:** Located in Lisle, this outdoor museum champions trees through science, conservation, and education.
- **State Snack Food:** Popcorn was designated the official snack food of Illinois in 2004.
- **Mormon History:** Nauvoo, Illinois was an important site in the history of the Mormon Church.
- **State Mineral:** Fluorite, known for its range of vibrant colors, was designated the state mineral in 1965.
- **Cahokia Mounds:** This archaeological site was once the most populous pre-Columbian city north of Mexico.
- **Garden of the Gods:** Located in the Shawnee National Forest, these rock formations provide scenic views and hiking trails.
- **Peoria:** Once considered the quintessential average American city, Peoria has a saying, "Will it play in Peoria?"
- **Chicago Fire of 1871:** This great fire killed hundreds and destroyed about 3.3 square miles of the city.
- **Bloomington-Normal:** This region is the proud home of State Farm Insurance and Beer Nuts.
- **The Great Migration:** Between 1916 and 1970, thousands of African Americans moved from the rural South to Chicago.
- **Mother Jones:** Activist and organizer Mary Harris "Mother" Jones is buried in the Union Miners Cemetery in Mount Olive.
- **State Amphibian:** The Eastern Tiger Salamander, known for its bright yellow or olive blotches, is the state amphibian.

- **Chicago Hot Dog:** A true Chicago-style hot dog is a beef frankfurter on a poppy seed bun, topped with a variety of condiments but never ketchup.
- **Kaskaskia Island:** This piece of land is the only part of Illinois located west of the Mississippi River.
- **Famous Author:** Ernest Hemingway was born in Oak Park, Illinois in 1899.
- **Buffalo Rock State Park:** This park on the Illinois River is home to two American bison.
- **The "I Will" Motto:** The motto of the city of Chicago is "I Will," a statement of resilience and determination.

Indiana

- **State Fossil:** The official state fossil is the horn coral, which lived in the warm shallow seas that once covered Indiana.
- **Indianapolis Motor Speedway:** This race track is the highest-capacity sports venue in the world, with a capacity of 400,000.
- **David Letterman:** Television host and comedian David Letterman was born in Indianapolis.
- **Jazz:** Indiana Avenue in Indianapolis was once a significant center for Jazz music, with many musicians getting their start there.
- **State Dance:** The square dance was designated as the official state dance in 1990.
- **Melissa Etheridge:** Grammy-winning singer-songwriter Melissa Etheridge was born in Leavenworth, Indiana.
- **State Soil:** Miami soil, a well-drained soil ideal for farming, is the state soil.
- **"Hoosier Hospitality":** This term refers to the warmth, friendliness, and kindness often associated with the residents of Indiana.
- **Kokomo Opalescent Glass:** Operating since 1888, it is the oldest manufacturer of hand-cast, hand-rolled opalescent and cathedral glass in the world.
- **Firefly Landing:** This children's museum in Terre Haute has a gallery designed by Bob Keeshan, better known as Captain Kangaroo.
- **State Rifle:** The Grouseland Rifle, made by Colonel John Small of Vincennes, was designated as the state rifle in 2012.
- **Larry Bird:** NBA legend Larry Bird was born in West Baden Springs and played college basketball for Indiana State.
- **Breaded Pork Tenderloin Sandwich:** This iconic Hoosier sandwich, with its large fried pork cutlet, is a staple in many Indiana restaurants.

- **Indiana Dunes National Park:** This national park on Lake Michigan's southern shore offers beaches, dunes, and over 50 miles of trails.
- **Evansville:** Known as "Pocket City," Evansville is Indiana's third-largest city and the largest city in Southern Indiana.
- **Historic Parke County:** This county has 32 covered bridges and has been the host of the Parke County Covered Bridge Festival since 1957.
- **Lafayette:** This city is home to Purdue University and is named for the French general Marquis de Lafayette.
- **Johnny Appleseed:** The gravesite of the legendary figure, real name John Chapman, is in Fort Wayne.
- **State Fruit:** The official state fruit is the watermelon, which is widely grown in southern Indiana.
- **Randy Moss:** Former NFL wide receiver Randy Moss played college football at Marshall, but was born in Rand, Indiana.

Iowa

- **Figge Art Museum:** This museum in Davenport, designed by British architect David Chipperfield, houses one of the Midwest's most significant collections of American art.
- **Ashton Kutcher:** This Hollywood actor, producer, and entrepreneur was born in Cedar Rapids, Iowa.
- **State Tree:** The official state tree is the Oak. It was chosen as the state tree in 1961 because of its abundance in the state.
- **National Mississippi River Museum & Aquarium:** This museum and aquarium in Dubuque is devoted to the culture and ecosystem of the Mississippi River.
- **Oldest Mosque:** The Mother Mosque of America, located in Cedar Rapids, is the oldest standing mosque in the U.S.
- **Red Delicious Apple:** This apple variety, one of the most famous in the world, was originally cultivated in Iowa.
- **Des Moines River:** This river, one of the two longest in the state, has been significant for transportation and water power since the 19th century.
- **Herky the Hawk:** The University of Iowa's mascot, Herky the Hawk, was created by Richard Spencer III in 1948.
- **Lewis and Clark Expedition:** The expedition camped on what is now the Iowa side of the Missouri River in 1804.
- **Crystal Lake:** Home to a statue of the world's largest bullhead fish.
- **Maquoketa Caves State Park:** This park is known for its collection of caves, some of which feature prehistoric Native American artwork.
- **Viking Lake State Park:** This popular camping spot is named after the Viking, which was the first European ship to reach North America.
- **Snake Alley:** Located in Burlington, it's often referred to as the most crooked street in the world.

- **Iowa Speedway:** Located in Newton, it's a state-of-the-art 7/8 mile asphalt paved tri-oval racetrack and motorsports facility.
- **Little Brown Church:** This historic church in Nashua was made famous by the song "The Church in the Wildwood".
- **Eliot Ness:** The famous law enforcement officer who led the "Untouchables," Eliot Ness, was born in Chicago, Illinois, but spent his final years in Coudersport, Pennsylvania.
- **National Sprint Car Hall of Fame & Museum:** Located in Knoxville, it's the only museum in the country dedicated to preserving the history of sprint car racing.
- **Sergeant Floyd Monument:** This monument in Sioux City is the first registered National Historic Landmark in the U.S.
- **'The Bridges of Madison County':** This famous novel and movie is set in Madison County, Iowa, which is home to six historic covered bridges.
- **Julien Dubuque's Mines:** These mines are part of a national monument honoring Julien Dubuque, who was one of the first European settlers in the area.

Kansas

- **Washunga Days:** This annual festival in Council Grove celebrates the culture of the Kaw people, a Native American tribe in the central United States.
- **State Bird:** The Western Meadowlark, known for its distinctive and melodic song, is the state bird of Kansas.
- **Keeper of the Plains:** A 44-foot tall steel sculpture in Wichita, it stands at the confluence of the Arkansas and Little Arkansas rivers.
- **Flyover State:** Kansas is sometimes referred to as a "flyover state," but its rich history and beautiful landscapes prove there's much to discover on the ground.
- **Salina:** Home to the Smoky Hill River Festival, one of the Midwest's largest art festivals.
- **Kansas Speedway:** A major motorsports venue in the U.S., Kansas Speedway in Kansas City hosts races from NASCAR to the ARCA Racing Series.
- **National Agricultural Center:** Bonner Springs is home to the National Agricultural Center and Hall of Fame, a museum dedicated to preserving the heritage of American agriculture.
- **Underground Vaults & Storage:** The world's largest underground storage facility is located in a salt mine in Hutchinson, Kansas, and is used to store everything from movie props to original film reels.
- **Leavenworth:** Known as the "First City of Kansas," Leavenworth was established in 1854 and is the location of the federal United States Penitentiary, Leavenworth.
- **Kansas State University:** The first land-grant college created under the Morrill Act was Kansas State University.
- **Famous Musicians:** Kansas has been the birthplace of many famous musicians, including jazz saxophonist Charlie Parker and rock singer Melissa Etheridge.

- **Big Well:** Located in Greensburg, the Big Well is the world's largest hand-dug well, reaching a depth of 109 feet.
- **Cowtown:** The Old Cowtown Museum in Wichita is an outdoor living history museum that recreates Wichita and Sedgwick County, Kansas, from 1865 to 1880.
- **Botanica Wichita:** This collection of gardens in Wichita spans 17.6 acres and includes over 4,000 species of plants.
- **Cessna and Beechcraft:** These two major aircraft manufacturers were both founded in Wichita, reinforcing the city's status as the "Air Capital of the World."
- **Rolling Hills Zoo:** Located in Salina, the zoo is unique for being located within a wildlife museum.
- **Barton County:** The county is the largest producer of oil in Kansas, with over 6,000 producing wells.
- **Tornadoes:** Kansas is part of "Tornado Alley" and experiences an average of 60 tornadoes annually.
- **Cheyenne Bottoms:** Located near Great Bend, it's the largest interior wetland in the U.S and a key layover point for North American migratory waterfowl.
- **Strataca:** This unique salt mine museum in Hutchinson takes visitors 650 feet below the Earth's surface to explore a 275 million-year-old salt deposit.

Kentucky

- **State Tree:** The Tulip Poplar, also known as the Yellow Poplar, is the state tree of Kentucky.
- **Pennyroyal Region:** This plateau region of Kentucky is known for its karst topography and abundant caves.
- **Blue Moon of Kentucky:** A bluegrass song written by Bill Monroe, it's one of the official state songs.
- **Kingdom Come State Park:** Named after the novel "The Little Shepherd of Kingdom Come," this state park features unique sandstone formations.
- **Natural Bridge State Resort Park:** Home to a natural sandstone arch that is 65 feet high and 78 feet long.
- **Zachary Taylor:** The 12th U.S. president, Zachary Taylor, was born in Barboursville, Kentucky.
- **Kentucky Opera:** Founded in 1952, the Kentucky Opera in Louisville is the state's premier opera company.
- **Bill Monroe:** Known as the "Father of Bluegrass," musician Bill Monroe was born in Rosine, Kentucky.
- **The Moonbow:** Cumberland Falls is one of the few places in the world where you can see a moonbow, a rainbow caused by the reflection of moonlight.
- **Covered Bridges:** Kentucky has over a dozen historic covered bridges, including the Switzer Covered Bridge, the state's oldest.
- **Mary Todd Lincoln:** The wife of President Abraham Lincoln, Mary Todd Lincoln, was born in Lexington, Kentucky.
- **The Kentucky Guild of Artists and Craftsmen:** The oldest statewide art and craft organization in Kentucky, it was founded in 1961.
- **Fort Harrod:** The first permanent settlement in Kentucky, Fort Harrod was founded in 1774.

- **Cave City:** Home to several notable attractions, including Mammoth Cave National Park and the aforementioned Wigwam Village.
- **State Insect:** The Honeybee is the state insect of Kentucky, recognized for its contribution to the state's agriculture.
- **Lost River Cave:** A seven-mile cave system in Bowling Green, Kentucky, which includes one of the largest natural entrances in the Eastern U.S.
- **State Fossil:** The Brachiopod, a marine shellfish that lived over 440 million years ago, is the state fossil of Kentucky.
- **My Morning Jacket:** This famous rock band was formed in Louisville, Kentucky, in 1998.
- **The Green River:** The beautiful Green River in Kentucky is a popular location for boating, fishing, and wildlife viewing.
- **Duncan Hines:** The man behind the famous line of baking products, Duncan Hines, was born in Bowling Green, Kentucky.

Louisiana

- **Beignets:** A popular deep-fried pastry, often served with powdered sugar at the famous Café du Monde in New Orleans.
- **Garden District:** A beautiful and historic neighborhood in New Orleans known for its well-preserved antebellum mansions.
- **Louisiana State Capitol:** The tallest state capitol building in the U.S., located in Baton Rouge.
- **Jean Lafitte:** A French pirate and privateer, Lafitte operated in the Gulf of Mexico and the New Orleans area in the early 19th century.
- **Swamp Pop:** A subgenre of pop music that originated in the Acadiana region in the 1950s.
- **Nicholls State University:** Located in Thibodaux, the university is named for Francis T. Nicholls, a former governor of Louisiana and member of the Louisiana Supreme Court.
- **Creole Cuisine:** A style of cooking originating in Louisiana, it combines influences from French, Spanish, West African, Amerindian, Haitian, German, Italian, British, and Irish cuisines.
- **Honey Island Swamp:** Considered one of the most pristine swampland habitats in the United States.
- **Frenchmen Street:** A popular strip in New Orleans known for its live music venues, particularly jazz.
- **Evangeline Oak:** A famous oak tree in St. Martinville associated with the Acadian heroine of Henry Wadsworth Longfellow's poem "Evangeline."
- **Louisiana Hayride:** A radio and later television country music show broadcast from the Shreveport Municipal Memorial Auditorium in Shreveport, Louisiana, that helped to launch the careers of some of the greatest names in American country and rockabilly music.
- **Tabasco Peppers:** These peppers, used to make Tabasco sauce, are primarily cultivated in Louisiana.

- **Rice Production:** Louisiana is one of the top rice-producing states in the U.S.
- **Cajun Zydeco Festival:** An annual celebration of Louisiana's unique music held in New Orleans.
- **Bourbon Street:** Known for its energetic nightlife, this historic street runs through the heart of New Orleans.
- **Lake Peigneur Disaster:** In 1980, a drilling mishap caused a lake to drain into a salt mine, creating a large whirlpool.
- **Pontchartrain Expressway:** A highway that stretches across the city of New Orleans.
- **Louisiana's Wetlands:** Louisiana's coastal wetlands make up about 40% of the United States' total wetland area.
- **The Sazerac:** Known as possibly the world's first mixed drink, it originated in New Orleans in the 19th century.
- **The Southern University:** Located in Baton Rouge, it's one of the largest historically black colleges or universities (HBCU) in the United States.

Maine

- **Lobster Festivals:** Maine is famous for its lobster festivals, including the Maine Lobster Festival in Rockland.
- **Wild Turkeys:** Wild turkeys, once wiped out in the state, now thrive in all of Maine's 16 counties.
- **Fryeburg Fair:** The state's largest agricultural fair, held annually in Fryeburg.
- **Skiing:** Maine is home to numerous ski resorts, including Sugarloaf and Sunday River.
- **Mount Desert Island:** The largest island off the coast of Maine, it's home to Acadia National Park.
- **Bates Mill Complex:** A historic textile factory complex in Lewiston, it's been redeveloped into a mixed-use complex.
- **Franco-American Culture:** Maine has a significant Franco-American population, particularly in the Lewiston-Auburn area.
- **Allagash Wilderness Waterway:** A 92-mile-long protected area offering some of the most remote canoeing experiences in the East.
- **Marginal Way:** A beautiful coastal walking path in Ogunquit, offering stunning ocean views.
- **Tom's of Maine:** A popular natural personal care products company founded in Kennebunk, Maine.
- **Wildlife Refuges:** Maine is home to several wildlife refuges, including the Rachel Carson National Wildlife Refuge.
- **Quoddy Head State Park:** The easternmost point of land in the U.S., home to the distinctive West Quoddy Head Light.
- **Maine Coon:** The official state cat, the Maine Coon, is one of the largest domesticated cat breeds.
- **Pemaquid Point Light:** Featured on the Maine state quarter, this lighthouse has an adjacent fisherman's museum.
- **Christmas Trees:** Maine is a significant producer of Christmas trees, with balsam fir being the most popular variety.

- **Wabanaki Tribes:** The indigenous peoples of Maine, including the Penobscot, Passamaquoddy, Mi'kmaq, and Maliseet tribes.
- **Cross Insurance Center:** An event venue in Bangor, it hosts concerts, conventions, and sports events.
- **Precipitation:** Maine has the highest average precipitation of any state in the northeastern U.S.
- **Thoreau-Wabanaki Trail:** This trail follows the routes taken by Henry David Thoreau and his Penobscot guides in the 1850s.
- **Moxie Festival:** An annual celebration in Lisbon, Maine, honoring the state's official soft drink.

Maryland

- **Deep Creek Lake:** Maryland's largest inland body of water, a hotspot for recreational activities.
- **Famous Filmmakers:** Famous film director John Waters is a native of Baltimore, Maryland.
- **Preakness Stakes:** Maryland hosts the annual Preakness Stakes, the second jewel in thoroughbred racing's Triple Crown.
- **George Peabody Library:** This library in Maryland is known for its stunning neo-greco interior architecture.
- **First Practical Refrigerator:** The first practical refrigerator was invented by Thomas Moore in Maryland in 1803.
- **Mount Clare Museum House:** The oldest colonial-era structure in Baltimore, it was completed in 1767.
- **Jousting Tournaments:** Maryland has held jousting tournaments since early colonial times, and it became the official state sport in 1962.
- **Babe Ruth:** The famous baseball player George Herman "Babe" Ruth was born in Baltimore, Maryland.
- **Great Falls:** The powerful and scenic rapids of the Potomac River, located in the Great Falls, are a sight to behold.
- **Firefighter Innovation:** The first mechanical firefighting unit in the U.S. was formed in Baltimore, Maryland.
- **Largest City:** Baltimore is the largest city in Maryland, with a rich history and vibrant culture.
- **Charm City:** Baltimore, Maryland's largest city, is affectionately known as "Charm City."
- **Scoville Scale:** Wilbur Scoville, who created the Scoville Scale for measuring the heat in peppers, was born in Maryland.
- **Chincoteague Oysters:** The world-famous Chincoteague Oysters come from Maryland's part of the Chincoteague Bay.
- **First Post Office:** The U.S. Postal Service was inaugurated in Baltimore, Maryland.

- **Famous Journalists:** Renowned journalists, including Connie Chung and David Simon, hail from Maryland.
- **Mallows Bay:** This bay in Maryland is known for its "Ghost Fleet," the largest collection of shipwrecks in the Western Hemisphere.
- **Blue Crabs:** The Chesapeake Bay Blue Crab, a Maryland icon, is a critical species for the local ecosystem and economy.
- **American Chestnut:** Maryland was once home to large populations of American Chestnut trees before the species was nearly wiped out by a fungal blight.
- **National Harbor:** The National Harbor in Maryland is a recent development and has become a major tourist destination.

Massachusetts

- **First Public Beach:** Revere Beach is the oldest public beach in the U.S.
- **Longest River:** The Connecticut River, which flows through four states, is the longest river in the New England region.
- **Blackstone River Valley:** Known as the "Birthplace of the American Industrial Revolution", this area features historical mill towns.
- **State Dance:** The official state dance of Massachusetts is the square dance.
- **Springfield Armory:** This National Historic Site produced military equipment from 1777 until its closing in 1968.
- **State Folk Hero:** Johnny Appleseed, a conservationist and apple tree planter, is the official state folk hero.
- **State Beverage:** The official state beverage of Massachusetts is cranberry juice, honoring the state's cranberry bogs.
- **State Game Bird:** The official state game bird of Massachusetts is the Wild Turkey.
- **Famous Composers:** Famous American composers like Leonard Bernstein and John Williams have connections to Massachusetts.
- **Oldest College Town:** The city of Cambridge is home to Harvard and MIT, making it the oldest college town in America.
- **The Charles River:** This river provides a popular site for rowing, sailing, and other outdoor activities in Boston.
- **Hasty Pudding Club:** This Harvard social club has been creating theatrical productions since 1844.
- **Concord Grapes:** The first Concord grapes were grown in Concord, Massachusetts, hence the name.
- **USS Massachusetts:** This World War II battleship is now a museum ship in Fall River.
- **State Dog Breed:** The official state dog of Massachusetts is the Boston Terrier.

- **Old Sturbridge Village:** This living museum depicts a rural New England town from the 19th century.
- **The "Codfish State":** Massachusetts is often referred to as the "Codfish State" due to its fishing industry.
- **State Marine Mammal:** The official state marine mammal of Massachusetts is the Right Whale.
- **The Big E:** The Eastern States Exposition, also known as The Big E, is the largest agricultural event on the eastern seaboard.
- **Lexington and Concord:** These towns are famous for their pivotal roles in the American Revolution.

Michigan

- **First Auto Traffic Tunnel:** The Detroit-Windsor Tunnel between the U.S. and Canada was the first traffic tunnel between two nations.
- **State Nickname:** Michigan's official nickname is "The Wolverine State."
- **Binder Park Zoo:** This Battle Creek zoo is one of the largest in Michigan, featuring a wide array of wildlife.
- **Cereal City:** Battle Creek is known as the "Cereal City" due to the headquarters of Kellogg's.
- **State Bird:** The official state bird of Michigan is the American Robin.
- **Lake St. Clair:** This lake between Ontario and Michigan is one of the busiest shipping channels in the world.
- **Michigan Dogman:** A cryptid that was first reported in 1887 in Wexford County.
- **Detroit Free Press Marathon:** One of few marathons in the world to cross international borders twice.
- **The Zehnder's Snowfest:** One of the top snow sculpting events in North America held annually in Frankenmuth.
- **Kalamazoo's Magic:** The town of Colon, near Kalamazoo, is known as the "Magic Capital of the World."
- **Ford's Theatre:** This is one of the world's premier historical theatres and it's located in Dearborn.
- **Michigan State Capitol:** Built in Lansing in 1872, it features a cast iron dome.
- **Detroit Lions:** Detroit's professional football team, they play at Ford Field in downtown Detroit.
- **Michigan Theatre:** The historical theater in Detroit is now a parking garage, but its opulent facade remains.
- **Rogers City:** Known as the Nautical City, this city hosts the world's largest limestone quarry.

- **Kellogg Brothers:** Both John Harvey and Will Keith, the founders of Kellogg's, were born in Battle Creek.
- **State Fish:** The Brook Trout is the official state fish of Michigan.
- **Leelanau Wine Trail:** This region is one of America's up-and-coming wine regions, with a unique microclimate ideal for vineyards.
- **Michigan Wines:** The state produces more than 2.5 million gallons of wine annually, ranking it in the top 10 wine producers in the U.S.
- **Historical Railroads:** The state is home to several historic railroads including the Adrian and Blissfield Rail Road Company.

Minnesota

- **Chisholm:** The birthplace of Greyhound Lines, Inc., it started as a hillybilly bus line between Hibbing and Alice.
- **The Jolly Green Giant:** The statue of the iconic mascot of the Green Giant Company stands in Blue Earth, Minnesota.
- **Laura Ingalls Wilder Museum:** This museum in Walnut Grove is dedicated to the author of the "Little House on the Prairie" books.
- **Split Rock Lighthouse:** This picturesque lighthouse is one of the most visited in the U.S.
- **Pequot Lakes:** Home to the notable Paul Bunyan Scenic Byway.
- **Hibbing High School:** Known for its architecture and size, it's also where Bob Dylan graduated.
- **Judy Garland Museum:** The birthplace of the "Wizard of Oz" star is in Grand Rapids, Minnesota.
- **Lake Superior:** The largest freshwater lake in the world by surface area is shared by Minnesota.
- **Cuyuna Country State Recreation Area:** A reclaimed mine pit now used for mountain biking, scuba diving, and fishing.
- **State Bird:** The common loon is Minnesota's state bird, known for its haunting calls.
- **Red Wing Shoes:** The international shoe brand was founded in Red Wing, Minnesota, in 1905.
- **International Wolf Center:** Located in Ely, it provides education and awareness about wolves and their behavior.
- **First Successful Open Heart Surgery:** The first successful open heart surgery was performed at the University of Minnesota in 1952.
- **Medtronic:** This medical device company, which made the first battery-operated external pacemaker, started in a Minneapolis garage.
- **Minnesota Zoo:** This Apple Valley zoo is renowned for its groundbreaking design and exhibits.

- **Charles Schultz:** The "Peanuts" comic strip creator was born and raised in Saint Paul.
- **Ojibwe Snowshoes:** The Ojibwe tribe, native to Minnesota, are believed to have designed the modern snowshoe.
- **State Motto:** The state motto of Minnesota is "L'Étoile du Nord," or "Star of the North."
- **Mesabi Iron Range:** One of the world's richest deposits of iron ore is found here.
- **Walleye:** This popular game fish is the state fish of Minnesota.

Mississippi

- **Shrimp and Petroleum Festival:** Despite the odd pairing, this is a real and popular festival in Morgan City.
- **Grenada Lake:** The largest body of water in the state, known for its excellent crappie fishing.
- **Great Mississippi River Balloon Race:** This annual hot air balloon event takes place in Natchez.
- **Watermelon Festival:** The town of Mize hosts this juicy festival each summer.
- **Mississippi Sandhill Crane:** The rarest crane species in North America can only be found here.
- **Blues Trail:** This series of markers throughout the state commemorates important locations in the history of blues music.
- **Gulf Coast:** Mississippi's Gulf Coast is a popular destination for beachgoers and seafood lovers.
- **Shepard State Park:** Named after astronaut Alan Shepard, this park is perfect for outdoor activities.
- **Roald Dahl:** The famous children's author was trained as a fighter pilot in Mississippi during World War II.
- **Mississippi State University:** This institution is recognized as a "high research activity" university.
- **Keesler Air Force Base:** This base in Biloxi is home to the 81st Training Wing of the U.S. Air Force.
- **Mississippi Agriculture & Forestry Museum:** This museum in Jackson showcases the history of agriculture in the state.
- **Kudzu:** Introduced to control soil erosion, this fast-growing plant has become a prominent part of Mississippi's landscape.
- **Mississippi River Commission:** Established in 1879, this commission seeks to improve navigation and prevent floods.
- **Mississippi Inland Paddling Trail:** This 123-mile paddling trail is the longest in the state.

- **Windsor Ruins:** The remains of the largest antebellum Greek revival mansion ever built in the state.
- **Tupelo Honey:** Named after Tupelo trees, this honey is among the highest quality in the world.
- **Moss Point:** Known for its beautiful Spanish moss-draped oaks.
- **Mississippi Petrified Forest:** This forest in Flora is one of only two in the eastern U.S.
- **Rosalie Mansion:** This pre-Civil War mansion in Natchez is a National Historic Landmark.

Missouri

- **Sliced Bread:** Chillicothe, Missouri, is the place where sliced bread was first sold in 1928.
- **"Meet Me in St. Louis":** This classic 1944 film starring Judy Garland is set in St. Louis at the time of the 1904 World's Fair.
- **Missouri Rhineland:** This region near the Missouri River is known for its vineyards and wineries.
- **Provel Cheese:** This cheese, a combination of Swiss, Provolone, and Cheddar, is a staple on St. Louis-style pizzas.
- **St. Joseph:** The starting point of the Pony Express and the death place of Jesse James.
- **Marceline:** Walt Disney spent part of his childhood in Marceline, which later influenced elements of Disneyland.
- **Soybeans:** Missouri is a major producer of soybeans in the U.S.
- **Bagnell Dam:** This dam created the Lake of the Ozarks when it was built in the 1920s.
- **Charlie Parker:** This influential jazz saxophonist was born in Kansas City, Missouri.
- **Titanic Museum:** Located in Branson, this museum is shaped like the famous ill-fated ship.
- **Hannibal:** This town is famous for being the childhood home of author Mark Twain.
- **Elephant Rocks State Park:** Named after the giant boulders that resemble a train of circus elephants.
- **Shel Silverstein:** The famed children's author and poet was born in St. Louis.
- **World War I Museum:** Kansas City is home to the National World War I Museum and Memorial.
- **Robert Pershing Wadlow:** Born in Alton, Missouri, he was the tallest person in recorded history.
- **Gooey Butter Cake:** A type of cake traditionally made in the St. Louis area.

- **Missouri Waltz:** Known as the state song, it gained fame as President Harry S Truman's favorite tune.
- **Route 66:** Many iconic sites of this historic highway can be found throughout Missouri.
- **Fantasy Baseball:** The first fantasy baseball league, Rotisserie League Baseball, started in St. Louis.
- **Precious Moments Chapel:** Located in Carthage, this chapel is filled with murals of the teardrop-eyed Precious Moments figurines.

Montana

- **Pompeys Pillar:** William Clark of the Lewis and Clark Expedition carved his name and the date in this rock in 1806.
- **Fresno Reservoir:** A popular fishing destination in north central Montana.
- **Ross Creek Cedars:** A scenic area home to western red cedars that are over 400 years old.
- **Whitefish Mountain Resort:** A popular ski resort on Big Mountain near Whitefish.
- **Kootenai Falls:** The largest undammed falls in the state.
- **Museum of the Rockies:** A Smithsonian Affiliate, recognized as one of the world's finest research and history museums.
- **Bozeman:** Known as "The Most Livable Place," Bozeman, Montana is renowned for its fly-fishing.
- **Montana's State Fossil:** The duck-billed dinosaur, known as Maiasaura peeblesorum, a large, herbivorous hadrosaur.
- **Billings:** The largest city in Montana, often called the "Magic City," because of its rapid growth as a railroad town.
- **Grizzly Bears:** The Lower 48's largest population of grizzly bears is found in Montana.
- **The Berkley Pit:** A former open pit copper mine in Butte, now one of the only places in the world where you can pay to see toxic waste.
- **The Montana Vortex:** A genuine quantum, or gravitational anomaly that may re-define the laws of physics and nature.
- **Little Bighorn Battlefield National Monument:** Preserves the site of the June 25 and 26, 1876, Battle of the Little Bighorn.
- **Montana's Personalities:** Actors Gary Cooper and Myrna Loy, musician Steve Albini, and author A.B. Guthrie are just a few noted personalities from Montana.
- **Evel Knievel Days:** An event held in Butte celebrating the famous motorcycle stuntman who hailed from the city.

- **International Wildlife Film Festival:** The first juried wildlife film festival in the world, held annually in Missoula.
- **Hyalite Canyon:** A popular outdoor recreational area south of Bozeman, including waterfalls, hiking trails, and rock and ice climbing.
- **Montana Cowboy Hall of Fame:** Located in Wolf Point, it's dedicated to honoring cowboys and ranching culture.
- **Swords Park:** A Billings park where you can see an overlook of four mountain ranges: the Pryor, Bighorn, Bull, and Beartooth.
- **Iceberg Lake:** A glacier-carved lake famous for its floating icebergs, located in Glacier National Park.

Nebraska

- **Nebraska's State Fossil:** The mammoth, a large, extinct relative of the elephant.
- **Johnny Rodgers:** The 1972 Heisman Trophy winner from the University of Nebraska is a legend in college football.
- **Hastings Museum:** The largest municipal museum in Nebraska features a planetarium and exhibits on natural and cultural history.
- **Homestead National Monument:** Commemorates the Homestead Act of 1862 and is located near Beatrice.
- **Union Pacific Railroad:** Founded in 1862, the company's headquarters have been in Omaha since 1867.
- **Lied Jungle:** Located in Omaha's Henry Doorly Zoo, it's one of the world's largest indoor rainforests.
- **Chadron State Park:** Nebraska's oldest state park, located in the picturesque Pine Ridge area.
- **Great Platte River Road Archway Monument:** A museum of westward expansion that spans across Interstate 80.
- **Malcolm X:** The civil rights leader was born in Omaha, and his birth site is now a historic landmark.
- **Marlon Brando:** The acclaimed actor's mother gave acting lessons to Henry Fonda in Omaha, where both actors were born.
- **Fontenelle Forest:** A 1,400-acre forest and nature center in Bellevue, just south of Omaha.
- **Toadstool Geologic Park:** Often compared to a lunar landscape, this unique park is in Nebraska's Panhandle.
- **Czech Heritage:** Nebraska has the highest percentage of residents with Czech ancestry in the U.S.
- **Bassett Lodge and Range Cafe:** Known as the "Cowboy Capital," Bassett is home to this rustic hotel and cafe.
- **Burlington Station:** This historic Omaha train station is now the home of local ABC affiliate KETV.

- **Daniel Freeman:** Recognized as the first person to file a claim under the Homestead Act, near Beatrice, Nebraska.
- **Sandhills Journey Scenic Byway:** A 272-mile route through the beautiful, dune-like Sandhills region of Nebraska.
- **Nebraska State Fair:** Held in Grand Island, it includes a large livestock competition and traditional fair attractions.
- **Standing Bear:** A Ponca chief, his court case in Omaha established that Native Americans are "persons within the meaning of the law."
- **Robert Taylor:** The Hollywood actor, known for films like "Camille" and "Waterloo Bridge," was born in Filley, Nebraska.

Nevada

- **Ghost Towns:** Nevada has more ghost towns than populated towns, remnants of its gold and silver mining past.
- **Lake Mead:** The largest reservoir in the U.S., formed by the Hoover Dam on the Colorado River.
- **Fallon Naval Air Station:** Home to the U.S. Navy's TOPGUN school, popularized in the Tom Cruise film.
- **Polar Bear Swim:** An annual New Year's Day tradition at Lake Tahoe's Zephyr Cove.
- **Pony Express Territory:** Part of the historic mail delivery route traversed what is now Nevada.
- **Gambling Legalization:** Nevada legalized gambling in 1931, creating the foundation for its major tourism industry.
- **Vegas Vic:** An iconic neon cowboy sign located on the Las Vegas Strip.
- **Frank Sinatra:** The famous singer's career revived in Las Vegas, where he became synonymous with the city's entertainment scene.
- **Mountain Bluebird:** Nevada's state bird, known for its striking blue color.
- **International Camel Races:** Held annually in Virginia City, a nod to the camels used in Nevada's mining days.
- **Elko Cowboy Poetry Gathering:** A week-long celebration of the cowboy life, including music, storytelling, and poetry.
- **Lamoille Canyon:** Known as the "Alps of Nevada," it's a scenic area in the Ruby Mountains.
- **Fly Geyser:** A colorful geothermal geyser on private land in Washoe County, only viewable by guided tour.
- **Moulin Rouge Hotel:** The first racially integrated hotel-casino in Las Vegas, opened in 1955.
- **Rhyolite Ghost Town:** This former gold mining town is one of the most photographed ghost towns in the West.

- **Creosote Bush:** One of the most common plants in Nevada's desert ecosystem, able to survive with little water.
- **High Roller:** Located in Las Vegas, it's the world's tallest observation wheel.
- **Ice Age Fossils:** The Tule Springs Fossil Beds National Monument in Las Vegas preserves Ice Age fossils.
- **Walker Lake:** One of the last remnants of an ancient inland sea, it's home to a unique species of cutthroat trout.
- **Mt. Moriah Wilderness:** This wilderness area in eastern Nevada is home to the state's second highest peak, Mt. Moriah.

New Hampshire

- **Isles of Shoals:** A group of small islands straddling the border between New Hampshire and Maine, known for their rugged beauty.
- **Appalachian Trail:** 161 miles of this famous long-distance hiking trail pass through New Hampshire.
- **Christmas Tree Farms:** The state has a thriving Christmas tree industry, with over 200 tree farms.
- **White Mountain National Forest:** Over 700,000 acres of mountainous landscape, a haven for hikers and outdoor enthusiasts.
- **Story Land:** A popular amusement park in Glen, based on classic children's fairy tales.
- **Wright Museum:** This Wolfeboro museum showcases WWII-era artifacts and exhibits.
- **Robert Frost Farm:** The home of renowned poet Robert Frost from 1900 to 1911, now a historic site and museum.
- **Polar Caves Park:** A set of ice age granite caves in the town of Rumney.
- **America's Stonehenge:** A controversial site in Salem, claimed to be ancient, possibly pre-Columbian, man-made structures.
- **Wildcat Mountain:** Offers one of the highest ski summits in New Hampshire and stunning views of Mount Washington.
- **Franklin Pierce:** 14th U.S. President, the only one from New Hampshire, known for his controversial pro-Southern stance.
- **Black Heritage Trail:** A walking tour in Portsmouth that highlights African American history from the 17th century to the modern civil rights era.
- **Alpine Slides:** New Hampshire has several, offering a unique and thrilling mountain descent experience.
- **Rye Harbor State Park:** A small coastal park with beautiful views, a favorite spot for whale watching.

- **Echo Lake:** A stunningly beautiful lake at the foot of Cannon Mountain, popular for swimming and picnicking.
- **Lupine Festival:** A yearly event celebrating the bloom of wild lupine flowers, held in Sugar Hill.
- **Piscataqua River:** One of the fastest tidal rivers in North America, it serves as the boundary between New Hampshire and Maine.
- **Daniel Webster:** This influential senator, diplomat, and orator was a native of New Hampshire.
- **Mallard Duck:** The state bird of New Hampshire, chosen for its abundance and familiarity to residents.
- **Squam Lake:** Used as the filming location for the classic movie "On Golden Pond."

New Jersey

- **High Point Monument:** The highest point in New Jersey, marked by a 220-foot obelisk.
- **Doo Wop Architecture:** Wildwood is famous for its 1950s and 1960s "Doo Wop" style motels.
- **Adventure Aquarium:** Located in Camden, it's a top attraction, particularly its massive shark tank.
- **Rutgers University:** One of the oldest colleges in the U.S., it's also the largest university in New Jersey.
- **Edwin Aldrin Birthplace:** The second man on the moon, Buzz Aldrin, was born in Montclair.
- **First Professional Basketball Game:** The first game was played in Trenton in 1896.
- **Ellis Island:** Though mostly associated with New York, a portion of Ellis Island is part of New Jersey.
- **Walt Whitman House:** The famous poet's home in Camden is now a museum.
- **Battleship New Jersey:** The most decorated battleship in U.S. Navy history is now a floating museum in Camden.
- **Historic Smithville:** A charming village with unique shops and boutiques located in Galloway.
- **New Jersey Symphony Orchestra:** Founded in 1922, it's one of America's leading orchestras.
- **George Washington Bridge:** One of the world's busiest bridges, connecting Fort Lee, New Jersey, and Manhattan.
- **Record Breaking Pizza:** The world's largest pizza was made in Norwood in 1998.
- **Meadowlands Sports Complex:** The site of numerous historic sports events, including Super Bowl XLVIII.
- **Corbin City:** Despite its name, it's one of the least populous municipalities in New Jersey.

- **Sandy Hook Lighthouse:** The oldest working lighthouse in the U.S., built in 1764.
- **Tuckerton Seaport:** A maritime village that celebrates New Jersey's coastal culture.
- **Zinc Mining History:** The Sterling Hill Mining Museum in Ogdensburg showcases this industry's past.
- **Cowtown Rodeo:** America's oldest running rodeo, located in Woodstown.
- **Bayonne Bridge:** The third longest steel arch bridge in the world, linking Bayonne to Staten Island.

New Mexico

- **Old Town Albuquerque:** The city's historic district dates back to the founding of the city in 1706.
- **The Lightning Field:** A land art installation of 400 stainless steel poles arranged in a grid.
- **Bisti/De-Na-Zin Wilderness:** Known for its striking and unusual eroded sandstone formations.
- **Elephant Butte Reservoir:** The largest lake in New Mexico, known for boating and fishing.
- **New Mexican Cuisine:** New Mexico is famous for its unique fusion of Pueblo Native, Spanish, Mexican, and American cuisines.
- **National Hispanic Cultural Center:** Based in Albuquerque, it's dedicated to the preservation, promotion, and advancement of Hispanic culture.
- **Los Alamos Scientific Laboratory:** The birthplace of the atomic bomb during World War II.
- **Ski Apache:** A popular ski resort on the slopes of Sierra Blanca Peak.
- **Spaceport America:** The world's first purpose-built commercial spaceport located in Sierra County.
- **Albuquerque International Balloon Fiesta:** An annual festival of hot air balloons that takes place in Albuquerque during early October.
- **Tinkertown Museum:** A quirky, self-built folk art museum located in Sandia Park.
- **The Burning of Zozobra:** A unique cultural event in Santa Fe where a giant marionette is burned to dispel the worries of the past year.
- **International Folk Art Market:** The world's largest international folk art market is held annually in Santa Fe.

- **Blue Hole, Santa Rosa:** An artesian well and popular scuba-diving spot with crystal-clear blue waters.
- **The Turquoise Trail:** A beautiful scenic byway linking Albuquerque and Santa Fe.
- **Ghost Ranch:** A 21,000-acre retreat and education center close to Abiquiu, made famous by painter Georgia O'Keeffe.
- **Kasha-Katuwe Tent Rocks:** Cone-shaped tent rock formations caused by volcanic eruptions 6 to 7 million years ago.
- **Mesilla:** A small town near Las Cruces, famous for its preserved adobe architecture.
- **Ruidoso Downs:** The home of the All American Futurity, the richest race in horse racing.
- **El Malpais National Monument:** Characterized by sandstone bluffs, this area showcases interesting volcanic features.

New York

- **Binghamton's Carousels:** Binghamton is home to six unique vintage carousels, gifted to the community in the 1920s and 1930s.
- **West Point:** The United States Military Academy is a prestigious and historic site located in West Point.
- **Letchworth State Park:** Known as the "Grand Canyon of the East," it's one of the most scenic areas in the eastern U.S.
- **Watkins Glen State Park:** Known for its impressive rock formations and 19 waterfalls along a narrow gorge.
- **Skaneateles Lake:** Known for its crystal clear, clean water, making it one of the cleanest lakes in the region.
- **Macy's Thanksgiving Day Parade:** The annual parade in New York City is the world's largest parade.
- **Montauk Point Lighthouse:** The oldest lighthouse in New York State, authorized by the Second Congress under President George Washington in 1792.
- **Albany's Egg:** An iconic concert venue known for its unusual egg-like design.
- **Bethel Woods Center for the Arts:** A performing arts center and museum located at the site of the 1969 Woodstock festival.
- **Sleepy Hollow:** This village inspired Washington Irving's story "The Legend of Sleepy Hollow."
- **Taughannock Falls State Park:** Home to a higher single-drop waterfall than Niagara Falls.
- **Great Appalachian Valley:** A major natural feature of eastern North America that includes the fertile Hudson Valley.
- **Seinfeld:** The famous sitcom was set in New York City, but most of it was filmed in Los Angeles.
- **Sagamore Hill:** Theodore Roosevelt's "Summer White House" is located on Long Island.

- **Whale Watching:** Long Island's coastal waters are a prime spot for whale watching.
- **Lake George:** Known as the "Queen of American Lakes," it's a popular destination for outdoor activities.
- **Canandaigua Lake:** Known for the large, historic mansions that line its shores.
- **Gansevoort Market:** A historic area in the Meatpacking District, known for its food hall and shopping venues.
- **Genesee River's High Falls:** A major waterfall located in the city of Rochester.
- **Boldt Castle:** Located on Heart Island in the Thousand Islands, it's a major landmark and tourist attraction.

North Carolina

- **Julian Price Memorial Park:** Covering 4,300 acres, it's the largest campground on the Blue Ridge Parkway.
- **North Carolina State Capitol:** Completed in 1840, it's one of the best-preserved examples of a Greek Revival-style public building.
- **Old Salem:** A historic district in Winston-Salem, it's a living history museum that recreates Moravian life in the 18th and 19th centuries.
- **The Mile High Swinging Bridge:** Located on Grandfather Mountain, it's America's highest suspension footbridge.
- **Carowinds:** A large amusement park, located on the border between NC and South Carolina.
- **Beech Mountain:** Eastern America's highest town, known for its skiing and mountain biking.
- **Elizabethan Gardens:** An English style garden located on Roanoke Island, created as a memorial to the first English colonists.
- **Linville Gorge:** Known as the "Grand Canyon of the East," it's one of the most scenic gorges in the eastern U.S.
- **North Carolina Symphony:** One of the world's longest-running orchestras, established in 1932.
- **New River:** One of the oldest rivers in the world, offering some of the best canoeing and kayaking in NC.
- **Great Dismal Swamp National Wildlife Refuge:** Despite its ominous name, it's a haven for wildlife.
- **Whitewater Falls:** The highest waterfall in the eastern U.S., located in the Nantahala National Forest.
- **Cherokee Foothills Scenic Byway:** Offers stunning views of the Blue Ridge Mountains and rich history of the Cherokee.
- **Reed Gold Mine:** Site of the first documented gold find in the U.S.
- **Sliding Rock:** A 60-foot natural rock slide in Pisgah National Forest that ends in a 7-foot deep pool.

- **Museum of the Cherokee Indian:** Offers an overview of 11,000 years of Cherokee history.
- **Battleship North Carolina:** The most decorated American battleship of WWII, now a war memorial in Wilmington.
- **Mount Airy:** Known as "Mayberry" due to its role as the inspiration for the town in the TV show "The Andy Griffith Show."
- **Linville Caverns:** NC's only show caverns, offering guided tours.
- **Durham Bulls Athletic Park:** Home to the famous minor league baseball team, the Durham Bulls.

North Dakota

- **State Fossil:** The Teredo Petrified Wood, an ancient wood that has transitioned to stone, is the state fossil.
- **Chateau de Mores:** A 26-room, hunting cabin-style chateau built by the Marquis de Morès in the 1880s.
- **Largest State Capitol Building:** North Dakota's state capitol is the tallest building in the state.
- **Missouri River:** North Dakota's section of the river offers excellent fishing and recreational opportunities.
- **Grahams Island State Park:** An ever-changing peninsula on Devils Lake, providing excellent outdoor activities.
- **North Country Trail:** The longest of the eleven National Scenic Trails, it passes through seven states including North Dakota.
- **Jamestown Reservoir:** A popular place for boating, fishing, camping, and bird-watching.
- **Diverse Wildlife:** North Dakota is home to many species of wildlife, including bison, pronghorn, and white-tailed deer.
- **Walhalla Border Crossing:** The second most northerly point on the U.S.-Canada border.
- **Pembina State Museum:** Offers a panoramic view of the Red River Valley from a 110-foot tower.
- **Souris River:** Known for its beauty, it's a major river in central and eastern North Dakota.
- **Red River Zoo:** Located in Fargo, it features species from around the world with an emphasis on cold climate species.
- **Dakota Zoo:** The state's largest zoo, located in Bismarck.
- **Valley City Bridges:** Known as the "City of Bridges" for its numerous railroad and other bridges.
- **Bottineau Winter Park:** Known as the "Jewel of the Turtle Mountains," it's a popular winter sports destination.
- **Rough Rider Hall of Fame:** Honors individuals who have brought fame to the state.

- **Fort Ransom State Park:** Offers a step back in time with a historical homesteading site.
- **Lewis and Clark Riverboat:** Offers cruises on the Missouri River.
- **World's Largest Sandhill Crane:** Named "Sandy," this statue stands in Steele, ND.
- **Minot State University:** Home to the Scandinavian Heritage Park.

Ohio

- **Cincinnati's Flying Pig Marathon:** A unique marathon named after the city's pork industry history.
- **Fountain Square:** A popular gathering place in downtown Cincinnati known for its historic Tyler Davidson Fountain.
- **Dayton Peace Accords:** The agreement to end the Bosnian War was negotiated in Dayton.
- **Glacial Grooves:** Geological features on Kelleys Island show the movement of glaciers thousands of years ago.
- **Chillicothe:** This city was Ohio's first state capital.
- **Wright-Patterson Air Force Base:** One of the largest and most diverse bases in the U.S. Air Force.
- **Akron Zips:** The University of Akron's sports teams are named after "zippers," which were mass-produced in Akron.
- **A Christmas Story House:** The house from the classic movie is located in Cleveland and is now a museum.
- **John Glenn:** The astronaut and U.S. Senator, the first American to orbit Earth, was from Cambridge, Ohio.
- **Fort Recovery:** The site of two significant American Indian battles, now a historical museum.
- **Erie Street Cemetery:** Cleveland's oldest existing cemetery, where many of the city's pioneers are buried.
- **Dorothy Fuldheim:** The first woman in the United States to anchor a television news broadcast, worked in Cleveland.
- **Blue Hole:** A natural artesian spring in Castalia that was once a popular tourist attraction.
- **Mound Builders:** Ohio was home to ancient mound-building cultures, and many of their earthworks are preserved.
- **Loveland Frog:** A local urban legend tells of a humanoid frog creature spotted in Loveland.

- **Great Lakes Science Center:** A museum in Cleveland dedicated to helping people learn about the environment of the Great Lakes.
- **Ohio State Fair:** One of the largest state fairs in the U.S., held in Columbus.
- **Shawnee State Forest:** Known as "The Little Smokies of Ohio," it's the state's largest state forest.
- **Underground Railroad:** Ohio was a crucial state in this network helping enslaved African Americans escape to freedom.
- **University of Cincinnati:** The university's DAAP program is consistently ranked as one of the most prestigious design schools in the U.S.

Oklahoma

- **Woolaroc Museum:** This museum and wildlife preserve was established by oilman Frank Phillips.
- **Spiro Mounds:** An important Mississippian culture archaeological site located in Spiro, Oklahoma.
- **The Blue Whale of Catoosa:** A famous roadside attraction along Route 66.
- **Pops 66 Soda Ranch:** A landmark on Route 66, known for its 66-foot tall soda bottle.
- **Sooner State:** The state's nickname, "Sooner State," comes from the settlers who claimed land "sooner" than was allowed.
- **Lake Eufaula:** Oklahoma's largest-capacity lake, often referred to as the "Gentle Giant."
- **Marland Mansion:** Known as the "Palace on the Prairie," this mansion showcases opulent 1920s architecture.
- **Bob Dunn:** A musician from Beggs, Dunn was the first guitarist to record with an electrically amplified instrument.
- **Gilcrease Museum:** Holds one of the world's most comprehensive collections of American Indian and Western art.
- **Vinita:** Founded in 1871, Vinita was the first town incorporated by the Oklahoma Territorial Legislature.
- **Hanson:** This Grammy-nominated pop-rock band, best known for their hit "MMMBop," hails from Tulsa.
- **Oklahoma Shakespeare in the Park:** A prominent outdoor theater company located in Oklahoma City.
- **Oklahoma City Zoo:** One of the oldest zoos in the U.S, it covers more than 110 acres.
- **Sam Noble Museum:** Home to the world's largest Apatosaurus skeleton.
- **Beaver Dunes Park:** Known as "Oklahoma's Little Sahara," a perfect location for off-road vehicle enthusiasts.

- **Heavener Runestone:** A mysterious stone with runic inscriptions, suggesting pre-Columbian Norse settlement.
- **Toy and Action Figure Museum:** Located in Pauls Valley, it's the first museum dedicated to action figures.
- **Archie Sam's Indian City USA:** An authentic replication of an American Indian village, located in Anadarko.
- **Mickey Mantle:** One of the greatest baseball players of all time, was born in Spavinaw, Oklahoma.
- **Oklahoma Opry:** A music hall in Oklahoma City, known for its live country music performances.

Oregon

- **The Rogue River:** Known for its salmon runs, whitewater rafting, and unmatched wildness.
- **Bottle Bill:** Oregon was the first U.S. state to enact a Bottle Bill (container-deposit legislation) in 1971.
- **Largest Organism:** The world's largest single living organism (a fungus) is in the Blue Mountains in Oregon.
- **Alpenrose Dairy:** A century-old dairy in Portland that's home to one of the world's smallest versions of a town, Dairyville.
- **Portland Aerial Tram:** It's one of only two commuter aerial trams in the U.S.
- **Evergreen Aviation Museum:** Home to the Spruce Goose, the largest airplane ever constructed.
- **Ghost Towns:** Oregon has more ghost towns than any other U.S. state.
- **Lincoln City's Kite Festival:** This annual event is one of the largest kite-flying festivals in the U.S.
- **Obsidian Flow:** The Big Obsidian Flow in the Newberry National Volcanic Monument is the youngest lava flow in Oregon.
- **Reed College:** Located in Portland, it is one of the most intellectual colleges in the country.
- **Columbia Sportswear:** Founded in 1938 in Portland, it is now a global brand selling outdoor wear and equipment.
- **Sunstone Gem:** The official state gem of Oregon and is found in the southeastern part of the state.
- **Hood River:** Known as the windsurfing capital of the world.
- **Mary's Peak:** The highest peak in the Oregon Coast Range with beautiful panoramic views.
- **Cycle Oregon:** An annual week-long bicycle tour held in different parts of Oregon.
- **Cape Perpetua:** A large forested headland on the Pacific coast of Oregon, with stunning coastal views.

- **Sisters:** A city in Deschutes County, named for the Three Sisters mountains just to the west.
- **Lake Oswego:** Known for its affluent citizens and its private lake.
- **Ecola State Park:** This scenic state park located on the Oregon coast is popular for hiking, surfing, and wildlife viewing.
- **Deschutes Brewery:** Based in Bend, it is the tenth-largest craft brewery in the U.S.

Pennsylvania

- **Reading Terminal Market:** One of America's largest and oldest public markets, found in Philadelphia.
- **Rockville Bridge:** The longest stone masonry arch railroad viaduct in the world, located in Harrisburg.
- **Lehigh Valley:** Known for its steel and cement industries, as well as its large health network.
- **Bushy Run:** Site of a 1763 battle between British troops and Native Americans during Pontiac's Rebellion.
- **Allegheny National Forest:** The only National Forest in Pennsylvania, a popular spot for outdoor recreation.
- **Pocono Mountains:** A popular recreational area for local and regional visitors with its resorts, lakes, and peaks.
- **Erie:** The only Great Lakes port in Pennsylvania, located on Lake Erie.
- **Wharton State Forest:** The largest state forest in the U.S., covering over 115,000 acres in the Pennsylvania Wilds.
- **Franklin Institute:** One of the oldest centers of science education in the U.S., located in Philadelphia.
- **Phipps Conservatory:** A complex of greenhouses in Pittsburgh, known for its botanical gardens and high-tech exhibits.
- **Blue Ball:** This town in Lancaster County is part of the Pennsylvania Dutch Country.
- **Knoebels Amusement Resort:** A free-admission amusement park in Elysburg, famous for its vintage roller coasters.
- **Eisenhower National Historic Site:** The home and farm of President Dwight D. Eisenhower, located in Gettysburg.
- **Moravian Pottery and Tile Works:** A National Historic Landmark in Doylestown, producing tiles in the Arts and Crafts tradition.
- **Independence Seaport Museum:** Dedicated to the maritime history of Philadelphia and the Delaware Valley.

- **Ricketts Glen State Park:** Famous for its old-growth forest and 24 named waterfalls.
- **Pennsylvania Tuxedo:** A term for traditional red-and-black checked hunting wear, named after its popularity in the state.
- **Fallingwater:** A famous house designed by architect Frank Lloyd Wright, partially built over a waterfall.
- **Shoofly Pie:** A molasses pie considered a traditional Pennsylvania Dutch dessert.
- **Liberty Bell Center:** The current home of the Liberty Bell, featuring exhibits on its history and impact.

Rhode Island

- **Thayer Street:** A popular shopping area in Providence, particularly among Brown University students.
- **South County:** This area, comprising several towns, is known for its stunning coastline and beaches.
- **Prescott Farm:** A historic farm in Middletown with structures dating back to the 18th century.
- **Benefit Street:** A historic street in Providence known for its high concentration of colonial buildings.
- **Athena, the Human-Robot Hybrid:** The first semi-autonomous humanoid robot built at Brown University.
- **Mohegan Bluffs:** Towering cliffs on Block Island, offering stunning ocean views.
- **The Towers:** An iconic historic structure in Narragansett, the remnant of the Narragansett Pier Casino.
- **Woonsocket:** This city has a significant French-Canadian heritage, visible in its architecture and culture.
- **H.P. Lovecraft:** The famed horror writer was born in Providence and his grave can be visited in Swan Point Cemetery.
- **Pell Bridge:** The longest suspension bridge in New England, spanning Newport Harbor.
- **Blackstone River Valley:** Known as the "Birthplace of the American Industrial Revolution."
- **Second Beach:** Officially known as Sachuest Beach, it's known for its scenic beauty and ideal surf conditions.
- **Rhode Island Philharmonic Orchestra:** A major cultural institution based in East Providence.
- **Herreshoff Marine Museum:** In Bristol, it's dedicated to the history of the Herreshoff Manufacturing Company.
- **Caserta Pizzeria:** A historic pizzeria in Providence known for its signature item, the Wimpy Skippy.

- **Roger Williams Park Zoo:** One of the oldest zoos in the country, it features over 100 species of rare animals.
- **Slatersville:** America's first planned industrial village, located in the town of North Smithfield.
- **Rhode Island Comic Con:** The biggest exhibition of its kind in the state, attracting thousands of visitors.
- **Tennis Hall of Fame:** Located in Newport, it's the world's largest museum dedicated to the sport of tennis.
- **Blithewold Mansion:** A 33-acre summer estate with its mansion, located in Bristol, that overlooks Narragansett Bay.

South Carolina

- **Bob Jones University Museum & Gallery:** It has one of the most recognized collections of European old masters in America.
- **"The Big Apple" Dance:** Originating in Columbia, it was a dance craze that spread across the U.S. in the 1930s.
- **Edisto Island Serpentarium:** A reptile zoo showcasing a variety of snake species.
- **Peachoid Water Tower:** A unique landmark in Gaffney, shaped and painted like a giant peach.
- **Aiken:** Known for its thoroughbred racing and training facilities.
- **Joe Riley Park:** Home of the Charleston RiverDogs, a minor league baseball team.
- **Avery Research Center:** Located in Charleston, it collects the history and culture of African Americans.
- **South Carolina State Museum:** The largest museum in the southeastern U.S., located in Columbia.
- **Allendale County:** It's the youngest county in South Carolina, having been formed in 1919.
- **South Carolina State House:** Located in Columbia, it's noted for its copper dome.
-
-
-
-
-
-
-
-
-
-

South Dakota

- **De Smet:** Known as "The Little Town on the Prairie", it is the home of the Ingalls family during the late 1800s.
- **American Bison:** The state animal of South Dakota, it's a symbol of the Great Plains.
- **Custer State Park:** Famous for its bison herds, scenic drives, and historic lodges.
- **Gavins Point Dam:** A hydroelectric dam on the Missouri River, it's one of six on the river.
- **Sitting Bull:** The famous Hunkpapa Lakota leader was born in South Dakota.
- **Black Hills Gold Rush:** A rush that took place in the 1870s and significantly influenced the history of the state.
- **Yankton:** The original capital of the Dakota Territory, before it was moved to Bismarck.
- **South Dakota Symphony Orchestra:** The premier musical organization in South Dakota, founded in 1922.
- **Brookings:** Home to South Dakota State University, the state's largest institution of higher education.
- **Sue:** The largest, most complete T-rex ever discovered was found near Faith, South Dakota.
- **Harney Peak:** The highest point in South Dakota and the highest peak east of the Rockies in the U.S.
- **Sioux Nation:** South Dakota is home to nine Sioux tribes, more than any other state.
- **Huron:** The city is the host of the South Dakota State Fair.
- **South Dakota Chislic:** A regional dish of cubed red meat most commonly from lamb or venison.
- **Missouri River:** The longest river in North America, it bisects South Dakota.
- **Bread and Circus Sandwich Kitchen:** A renowned eatery in Sioux Falls known for its homemade sandwiches.

- **Terry Redlin:** An American artist known for his painted rural and wildlife scenes, was born in Watertown.
- **Sisseton:** Named for the Sisseton division of the Native American Sioux, known for its hills and bodies of water.
- **Watertown:** Home to the Redlin Art Center which houses most of the original art of Terry Redlin.
- **Bramble Park Zoo:** Located in Watertown, it features a diverse living collection of animals from around the world.

Tennessee

- **The Old Mill:** A historic grist mill in Pigeon Forge, it's been in continuous operation since 1830.
- **Raccoon Mountain Caverns:** More than five miles of caverns and underground passageways located in Chattanooga.
- **Nashville Hot Chicken:** A local specialty, this fried chicken dish is known for being seasoned with a spicy paste.
- **Iroquois Steeplechase:** An annual horse racing meet in Nashville, dating back to 1941.
- **Cumberland Gap:** A significant pass through the Appalachian Mountains, used by Native Americans and pioneers.
- **Country Music Hall of Fame:** A large museum in Nashville dedicated to preserving the history of country music.
- **Tennessee Williams:** The famous American playwright was born in Mississippi but his family moved to Tennessee, hence his name.
- **Tennessee Volunteers:** The University of Tennessee's athletic teams, known for their distinctive orange and white uniforms.
- **Reelfoot Lake:** A shallow natural lake in northwest Tennessee, created by a series of earthquakes in 1811-12.
- **Memphis Brooks Museum of Art:** The oldest and largest art museum in the state of Tennessee.
- **Frist Art Museum:** Located in Nashville, it's housed in the city's former main post office building.
- **Tennessee State Capitol:** The state capitol building in Nashville, it's one of the oldest working capitols in the US.
- **Market Square, Knoxville:** A pedestrian mall listed on the National Register of Historic Places.
- **Natchez Trace Parkway:** A scenic road through Tennessee, Alabama, and Mississippi, it follows a historic Native American trail.

- **James K. Polk Ancestral Home:** The home of the 11th U.S. president, located in Columbia.
- **Johnny Cash Museum:** Located in Nashville, it's dedicated to the life and music career of the "Man in Black".
- **Cheekwood Estate & Gardens:** A 55-acre botanical garden and art museum located on the historic Cheek estate in Nashville.
- **Percy Warner Park:** One of the largest municipal parks in Tennessee, located in Nashville.
- **American Museum of Science and Energy:** Located in Oak Ridge, it provides a narrative of the WWII Manhattan Project.
- **Stax Museum:** Located in Memphis, it's dedicated to preserving the legacy of soul music, particularly that of Stax Records.

Texas

- **Texas Independence Day:** March 2nd marks the celebration of Texas' independence from Mexico.
- **Texas Hill Country:** Known for its rolling hills and wineries.
- **Blue Bell Creameries:** The popular ice cream brand was founded in Brenham, Texas.
- **South by Southwest (SXSW):** An annual conglomerate of film, interactive media, and music festivals and conferences in Austin.
- **Mariano Martinez:** The Dallas restaurateur invented the frozen margarita machine.
- **King of Country:** George Strait, often referred to as the "King of Country", is from Poteet, Texas.
- **NASA's Johnson Space Center:** Located in Houston, it's the lead center for human spaceflight operations.
- **The Painted Churches of Texas:** A series of historical churches, painted by German and Czech immigrants.
- **Whataburger:** The popular fast-food chain was founded in Corpus Christi.
- **The Kilgore Rangerettes:** The world's first college dance drill team, founded in Kilgore, Texas.
- **Texas Medical Center:** The largest medical complex in the world, located in Houston.
- **The Yellow Rose of Texas:** An iconic symbol of Texas, stemming from an 1858 song.
- **Janis Joplin:** The legendary rock singer was born in Port Arthur, Texas.
- **Cadillac Ranch:** A public art installation featuring ten Cadillacs buried nose-first in Amarillo.
- **ZZ Top:** The rock band known for their long beards hails from Houston.
- **Dallas/Fort Worth International Airport:** The second largest airport by area in the United States.

- **Pecan Tree:** The state tree of Texas, the pecan tree is native to the state.
- **Sam Houston:** One of the most important figures in Texas history, Houston served as the first and third president of the Republic of Texas.
- **Big Tex:** A 55-foot tall statue and cultural icon, located at the grounds of the State Fair of Texas.
- **Lyndon B. Johnson Space Center:** NASA's center for human spaceflight, where astronauts train for missions.

Utah

- **Antelope Island:** The largest island in the Great Salt Lake, home to a large population of bison.
- **Skiing:** Utah's license plates advertise "the Greatest Snow on Earth".
- **Provo:** Home to Brigham Young University, one of the largest private higher education institutions in the U.S.
- **Quaking Aspen:** The state tree, notable for its trembling leaves.
- **Capitol Reef National Park:** Known for its white sandstone cliffs, canyons, and domes.
- **Utah Olympic Park:** A winter sports park built for the 2002 Winter Olympics.
- **Seagull Monument:** Commemorates the Miracle of the Gulls, where seagulls saved the Mormon pioneers' first harvest in Utah.
- **The Osmonds:** The famous family musical group hails from Ogden, Utah.
- **Flaming Gorge National Recreation Area:** Known for its deep blue reservoir and dramatic red cliffs.
- **Pando Forest:** One of the oldest and largest organisms, a single clonal colony of quaking aspen.
- **Goblin Valley State Park:** Known for its thousands of hoodoos, referred to locally as "goblins".
- **Bonanza:** The longest-running western TV series in U.S. history was filmed in Utah.
- **Cedar Breaks National Monument:** Home to a natural amphitheater, stretching across 3 miles, with a depth of over 2,000 feet.
- **Blue John Canyon:** Famous from the movie "127 Hours", which is based on Aron Ralston's survival story.
- **Slickrock Bike Trail:** A popular mountain biking destination in Moab.

- **Utah Symphony:** One of the only American orchestras that perform 52 weeks a year.
- **Lone Peak Wilderness:** Known for its rugged mountain views and glacial valleys.
- **Four Corners Monument:** Utah is one of the four states (Utah, Colorado, New Mexico, and Arizona) meeting at this point.
- **Timpanogos Cave National Monument:** A cave system in the Wasatch mountains.
- **Pioneer Day:** State holiday celebrated on July 24th, marking the day that Brigham Young and the first Mormon pioneers arrived in Salt Lake Valley in 1847.

Vermont

- **Neshobe River:** The Longest river entirely within Vermont.
- **Rock of Ages Quarry:** One of the largest granite quarries in the world, located in Barre.
- **Vermont Law School:** The top-ranked environmental law school in the United States.
- **Burlington Coat Factory:** Despite its name, the retailer originated in Burlington, New Jersey, not Vermont.
- **Green Up Day:** An annual state-wide event where volunteers clean up roadside trash.
- **Brattleboro Retreat:** One of the oldest mental health hospitals and the largest employer in Southern Vermont.
- **Burlington Bike Path:** A scenic waterfront path that offers stunning views of Lake Champlain.
- **Covered Bridges:** Vermont has over 100 covered bridges, more per square mile than any other U.S. state.
- **Vermont State House:** One of the oldest and best preserved of our nation's state capitols.
- **Missisquoi National Wildlife Refuge:** Covers 6,729 acres of wetlands on the eastern shore of Lake Champlain.
- **The Vermont Country Store:** An iconic retail business that specializes in hard-to-find goods and Vermont-made products.
- **Eugenics Survey:** In the early 20th century, Vermont was the site of a controversial eugenics survey aimed at isolating and sterilizing "degenerate" residents.
- **Highest Elevation:** Mount Mansfield is the highest mountain in Vermont with a summit that peaks at 4,393 feet above sea level.
- **First in Voting:** Vermont was the first state to grant partial voting rights to women in 1880.
- **Statehood:** Became the 14th state to join the Union on March 4, 1791.

- **First Ski Tow:** The first ski tow in the United States was created in Woodstock, Vermont in 1934.
- **Landlocked Salmon:** Lake Champlain is home to landlocked Atlantic salmon, a unique subspecies that has adapted to freshwater living.
- **French Influence:** Many towns in Vermont have French names due to the early presence of French settlers and explorers.
- **Conservation Movement:** Vermont has been a leader in the U.S. conservation movement, with numerous state parks and nature preserves.
- **Hermit Thrush:** The hermit thrush, known for its beautiful song, is Vermont's state bird.

Virginia

- **Virginia Military Institute:** The oldest state-supported military college in the U.S.
- **The American Civil War:** Virginia saw more battles during the Civil War than any other state.
- **The Appalachian Plateau:** Virginia's portion of this plateau is known for its coal mining.
- **Old Dominion:** Nickname for Virginia, given because it was the first colonial possession established in mainland British America.
- **Fairfax County:** The most populous county in Virginia, and home to several influential federal agencies.
- **George Mason University:** The largest public research university in the state of Virginia.
- **Langley Air Force Base:** One of the oldest airfields continuously used by the U.S. Air Force.
- **Fort Monroe:** A military installation located on Old Point Comfort, known as Freedom's Fortress.
- **Dogwood:** The state flower and tree of Virginia.
- **First English Child:** Virginia Dare, the first child of English parents born in the New World, was born in Virginia.
- **Smithsonian's National Air and Space Museum Steven F. Udvar-Hazy Center:** The companion facility to the museum on the National Mall, it displays thousands of aviation and space artifacts.
- **Mariners' Museum and Park:** One of the largest maritime museums in North America.
- **Agriculture:** Virginia is the nation's third largest producer of seafood, and its vineyards are within the top 10 in wine production.
- **Natural Bridge:** A geological formation in Rockbridge County that forms a 215-foot high natural bridge.

- **Grey Fox:** The state mammal, found in the mountains and forests of Virginia.
- **Manassas National Battlefield Park:** The site of two major American Civil War battles.
- **Norfolk Naval Shipyard:** One of the largest shipyards in the world, specializing in repairing, overhauling, and modernizing ships and submarines.
- **The Homestead:** The birthplace of American spa culture, with hot springs in use for over two centuries.
- **Virginia State Route 110:** Offers an iconic view of the Pentagon and Washington D.C.'s monuments.
- **Busch Gardens Williamsburg:** A 383-acre theme park with a European theme, including areas representing England, France, Germany, Italy, Scotland, and Ireland.

Washington

- **The Gorge Amphitheatre:** A concert venue offering a spectacular view of the Columbia River.
- **Seattle Seahawks:** The 2014 Super Bowl Champions.
- **Vashon Island:** The island is accessible only by ferry and has no bridge to the mainland.
- **Rain Shadow Effect:** The Olympic Mountains create a significant rain shadow, making the western side much wetter than the east.
- **Orcas Island:** The largest of the San Juan Islands, known for its resident pods of orcas.
- **Port Townsend:** Known for its Victorian architecture, the city is a designated National Historic Landmark District.
- **Sasquatch!:** An annual music festival held at the Gorge Amphitheatre.
- **Washington State Capitol:** The legislative building's dome is the fifth tallest masonry dome in the world.
- **Fremont Troll:** An iconic public sculpture in the Fremont neighborhood of Seattle.
- **International Kite Festival:** Held annually in Long Beach, it's one of the premier kite-flying events in the world.
- **Fort Worden Historical State Park:** The 434-acre park includes over 2 miles of saltwater shoreline and a wide variety of services and facilities.
- **Museum of Pop Culture:** The museum houses exhibits that cover pop culture, from the art of fantasy, horror cinema, and video games to science fiction literature and costumes from screen and stage.
- **Gas Works Park:** The park incorporates numerous pieces of the old plant, some of which are still operational, providing a fascinating insight into the industrial history of the region.
- **Alki Point:** It was the landing site of the first white settlers in Seattle.

- **The Tacoma Dome:** One of the largest wood domed structures in the world.
- **Chateau Ste. Michelle:** Washington State's founding winery featuring award-winning wines.
- **Nordic Heritage Museum:** The only museum in the United States to honor the legacy of immigrants from the five Nordic countries.
- **Boeing Everett Factory:** The world's largest building by volume, where jumbo jets like the 747, 767, 777, and 787 are assembled.
- **Bumbershoot:** An international music and arts festival held in Seattle every Labor Day weekend.
- **Snoqualmie Falls:** A 268-foot waterfall on the Snoqualmie River, visited by 1.5 million people each year.

West Virginia

- **The Graceland Inn:** Located on the Davis & Elkins College campus, this historic landmark inn offers Victorian-era elegance.
- **Appalachian Power Park:** Home of the West Virginia Power, a minor league baseball team.
- **Prickett's Fort State Park:** A recreated rustic fort on the banks of the Monongahela River, offering a glimpse into the past.
- **Droop Mountain Battlefield:** The site of West Virginia's last significant Civil War battle.
- **West Virginia State Museum:** Tells the story of West Virginia through exhibits ranging from prehistoric times to the present day.
- **Wheeling Suspension Bridge:** The oldest operating suspension bridge in the world.
- **Lost World Caverns:** A series of underground natural caves located in Lewisburg.
- **Huntington:** Known for its vibrant arts scene, it's the second-largest city in West Virginia.
- **Gauley River:** Renowned for its whitewater rafting, considered some of the best in the world.
- **Beckley Exhibition Coal Mine:** A restored coal mine where visitors can learn about the history of coal mining.
- **West Virginia State Fair:** Held annually in Lewisburg, featuring concerts, agricultural competitions, and carnival rides.
- **Tamarack:** The largest retailer of West Virginian craft products, such as handmade quilts, and art.
- **Green Bank Telescope:** The world's largest fully steerable radio telescope.
- **West Virginia Strawberry Festival:** Held annually in Buckhannon, it's a unique, traditional celebration.
- **Cass Scenic Railroad State Park:** Home to the world's largest fleet of geared Shay locomotives.

- **George Washington National Forest:** The forest covers 1.8 million acres of land, making it one of the largest tracts of public land in the Eastern U.S.
- **Pearl S. Buck Birthplace:** The childhood home of the Pulitzer and Nobel Prize-winning author.
- **Grafton National Cemetery:** The final resting place for thousands of Union soldiers, and the site of the first nationwide observance of Memorial Day.
- **Snowshoe Mountain:** A major ski resort offering year-round activities.
- **National Radio Astronomy Observatory:** One of the world's premier radio observatories, located in the small town of Green Bank.

Wisconsin

- **Bucky Badger:** The beloved mascot of the University of Wisconsin-Madison.
- **Ellsworth Cooperative Creamery:** Known as the Cheese Curd Capital of Wisconsin.
- **Summerfest:** Known as "The World's Largest Music Festival," held annually in Milwaukee.
- **Kohler Company:** The famous plumbing product manufacturer is based in Kohler, Wisconsin.
- **Horicon Marsh:** The largest freshwater cattail marsh in the U.S.
- **Monroe:** Known as the Swiss Cheese Capital of the World.
- **Devil's Lake State Park:** The most visited state park in Wisconsin, attracting over 3 million visitors per year.
- **Wisconsin State Bird:** The American robin, recognized for its cheery song and early appearance in spring.
- **Kettle Moraine State Forest:** Its unique glacial features attract visitors from around the world.
- **Cave of the Mounds:** A National Natural Landmark, known for its beautiful stalactites, stalagmites, and other mineral formations.
- **The Dells of the Wisconsin River:** A 5-mile gorge noted for its scenic beauty and the unique Cambrian sandstone formations along its banks.
- **Madison:** Wisconsin's capital city, known for its vibrant cultural scene and beautiful setting between two lakes.
- **Wisconsin State Tree:** The sugar maple, an important part of Wisconsin's economy for its sap.
- **The Wisconsin Idea:** A policy developed at the University of Wisconsin that the university should improve people's lives beyond the classroom.
- **Wisconsin State Dog:** The American water spaniel, a breed developed in the state.

- **Dr. Evermor's Forevertron:** The world's largest scrap metal sculpture, located in North Freedom.
- **Beloit Snappers:** A Minor League Baseball team that plays in the High-A Central league.
- **Marquette University:** A private Jesuit university located in Milwaukee, the largest private university in Wisconsin.
- **Sargento:** The first company to sell packaged shredded cheese, based in Plymouth, Wisconsin.
- **The National Mustard Museum:** Located in Middleton, it showcases a collection of over 6,000 mustards from all 50 U.S. states and over 70 countries.

Wyoming

- **State Dinosaur:** Triceratops, which roamed parts of Wyoming during the late Cretaceous period, is Wyoming's state dinosaur.
- **Buffalo Bill Cody:** The city of Cody, founded by the famous Wild West figure, offers a rich exploration of western American history.
- **Bighorn Sheep:** The state's official mammal, Wyoming is home to one of the largest herds in the U.S.
- **Moose:** The largest species in the deer family, moose are common in Wyoming's mountain areas.
- **Petrified Forest:** Found within Yellowstone National Park, this ancient forest turned to stone is a popular attraction.
- **Hell's Half Acre:** An eerie, otherworldly landscape used as a location for the sci-fi movie "Starship Troopers."
- **Union Pacific's Big Boy:** The world's largest steam locomotive, restored and displayed in Cheyenne.
- **Fossil Butte National Monument:** Known as "America's Aquarium in Stone," it has some of the world's best preserved fossils.
- **Wyoming State Museum:** Located in Cheyenne, the museum showcases the state's cultural, geological, and natural history.
- **Casper Mountain:** A popular outdoor destination offering year-round recreational activities.
- **Seedskadee National Wildlife Refuge:** A sanctuary for over 200 species of birds, located on the Green River.
- **Shoshone National Forest:** The first National Forest in the U.S., set aside as part of the Yellowstone Timberland Reserve in 1891.
- **Jenny Lake:** A picturesque lake located at the foot of the Teton Range, it's a beloved spot for hikers and boaters.
- **Chugwater:** The town is famous for its chili, culminating in an annual cook-off that draws competitors from across the region.
- **Coal Mines:** The state is home to some of the world's largest open pit coal mines.

- **Wild West History:** Wyoming has been the site of many of the most famous events in Wild West lore, including cattle wars and infamous outlaws.
- **Ranching:** Wyoming's largest industry is agriculture, and beef is its top agricultural product.
- **Medicine Wheel/Medicine Mountain National Historic Landmark:** This ancient Native American stone structure continues to be a site of ceremony and spirituality.
- **Sundance:** The town where the Sundance Kid got his nickname.
- **Nellie Tayloe Ross:** Elected in 1924, Ross was the first woman governor in the U.S., serving Wyoming.

Conclusion

As we close the final pages of the third volume of "1000 Facts about The United States of America," we reach the end of an incredible voyage. This journey through the fifty states has allowed us to delve into the intricacies of America's rich history, diverse cultures, remarkable landscapes, impressive innovations, and so much more.

We have celebrated the creativity and resilience that have shaped this nation, from the revolutionary spirit that breathed life into its independence, to the scientific advancements that have placed it at the forefront of global progress. We have ventured into the heart of America's cities and traversed its sweeping rural landscapes, appreciating the enduring beauty and resourcefulness that define the nation.

Through these 1000 fascinating facts, we've sought to encapsulate the essence of the United States, a nation marked by its vibrant cultural mosaic, its relentless pursuit of progress, and its unwavering spirit of liberty. We have highlighted the triumphs, acknowledged the tribulations, and, above all, celebrated the indefatigable spirit that characterizes the American people.

As we conclude, it's important to remember that every fact has served as a thread in the grand tapestry that is America. Each one contributes to the larger narrative that binds these fifty states into one extraordinary nation.

As we part ways, we encourage you to continue exploring, for the beauty of knowledge lies in its ceaseless pursuit. Keep learning, keep discovering, and remember - America, in all its complexity and dynamism, will never cease to amaze.

Daniel Scott

www.ingramcontent.com/pod-product-compliance
Lightning Source LLC
Chambersburg PA
CBHW050736260726
48661CB00001B/269